S0-EIL-783

Nontariff Barriers to High-Technology Trade

Westview Special Studies

The concept of Westview Special Studies is a response to the continuing crisis in academic and informational publishing. Library budgets are being diverted from the purchase of books and used for data banks, computers, micromedia, and other methods of information retrieval. Interlibrary loan structures further reduce the edition sizes required to satisfy the needs of the scholarly community. Economic pressures on university presses and the few private scholarly publishing companies have greatly limited the capacity of the industry to properly serve the academic and research communities. As a result, many manuscripts dealing with important subjects, often representing the highest level of scholarship, are no longer economically viable publishing projects—or, if accepted for publication, are typically subject to lead times ranging from one to three years.

Westview Special Studies are our practical solution to the problem. As always, the selection criteria include the importance of the subject, the work's contribution to scholarship, and its insight, originality of thought, and excellence of exposition. We accept manuscripts in camera-ready form, typed, set, or word processed according to specifications laid out in our comprehensive manual, which contains straightforward instructions and sample pages. The responsibility for editing and proofreading lies with the author or sponsoring institution, but our editorial staff is always available to answer questions and provide guidance.

The result is a book printed on acid-free paper and bound in sturdy library-quality soft covers. We manufacture these books ourselves using equipment that does not require a lengthy make-ready process and that allows us to publish first editions of 300 to 1000 copies and to reprint even smaller quantities as needed. Thus, we can produce Special Studies quickly and can keep even very specialized books in print as long as there is a demand for them.

About the Book

This book describes European and Japanese nontariff barriers (NTBs) in areas of high-technology trade and discusses their impact on the international behavior of U.S. firms. This study was prompted by the rising incidence of nontariff measures in high-technology sectors, as governments increasingly attempt to promote the growth of new industries through various domestic subsidy policies and import protection. As applied in high-technology sectors, protectionism typically includes discriminatory government procurement, incompatible standards and product certification procedures, performance requirements, import licensing, and a failure to protect intellectual property.

The authors use case histories to explore the incidence and impacts of these nontariff measures. Impacts are described in company-specific terms and include, for example, company efforts to redeploy research and development activities within the protected market, thus stimulating increased transfer of technology; alteration of product characteristics and the direction of research and development to satisfy local specifications; joint venturing with local partners, as well as with larger U.S. firms with an established market position; and abandoning the market entirely. The book includes a number of policy recommendations designed to reorient international trade negotiations toward the wide range of nontariff barrier impacts and the particular difficulties that smaller firms have in dealing with import restrictions.

Nontariff Barriers to High-Technology Trade

Robert B. Cohen, Richard W. Ferguson, and Michael F. Oppenheimer

Westview Press / Boulder and London

Westview Special Studies in International Economics and Business

Published in 1985 in the United States of America by Westview Press, Inc., Frederick A. Praeger, Publisher, 5500 Central Avenue, Boulder, Colorado 80301

Library of Congress Catalog Card Number: 85-8829
ISBN: 0-8133-7075-2

Composition for this book was provided by the authors
Printed and bound in the United States of America

6 5 4 3 2 1

Contents

About the Authors

Michael F. Oppenheimer is Vice President for International Programs at The Futures Group, with principal responsibilities for marketing, project management and corporate policy in the international field. Mr. Oppenheimer has managed projects on North-South negotiations, U.S. technology transfer policy, future strategic issues, and U.S. trade policy with respect to export credit subsidies and high-technology trade. He is currently at work on a major study of Japanese and European industrial policy, as well as further research on Japanese and European high-technology trade barriers. He has consulted for the Departments of Commerce and State, the U.S. Trade Representative, the Office of Science and Technology Policy, the Office of Technology Assessment, as well as numerous private firms. He is co-author of books on the U.S. Export-Import Bank and on U.S. diplomacy in global conferences. Prior to joining The Futures Group, he was international relations advisor to the General Accounting Office and did graduate work in foreign policy at the University of Virginia.

Robert B. Cohen is an expert on international industrial competition. He has done extensive work on the auto, computer and software industries for the MIT Future of the Automobile Program, the United Nations and the Congress' Office of Technology Assessment. Dr. Cohen has written extensively on the international debt crisis and multinational firms. He is the author of volumes on foreign investment in the United States and services and corporate headquarters, and coeditor of the posthumous collection of Stephen Hymer's writings on the multinational corporation. At present, he is a special consultant on high-technology economic development programs for the New York State Urban Development Corporation. He was previously Senior International Economist at The Futures Group.

Richard W. Ferguson, a political economist, is currently working on West German monetary policy under a Fulbright grant. Prior to this, Mr. Ferguson was a staff research associate in The Futures Group's International Division. He has specialized in international economic and financial issues, with particular emphasis on the European economies. He also conducted substantial research on European security matters. He received an MA in international relations from the Johns Hopkins School of Advanced International Studies.

Nontariff Barriers to High-Technology Trade

Executive Summary

CONCLUSIONS

1. Nontariff barriers (NTBs) have gained increasing prominence as commercial and diplomatic issues. The significant reductions in tariffs achieved during a succession of GATT-sponsored trade negotiations exposed NTBs previously obscured by high tariff levels. They also have induced countries to adopt nontariff measures to protect those industries deprived of tariff protection. These negotiations have broadened our definition of what constitutes a trade barrier to encompass development and industrial policy instruments previously defined as domestic. Finally, the secular decline of mature industries in the developed countries has stimulated protectionist pressures and the imposition of nontariff barriers to ease the adjustment burden and to promote new sectors that are expected to be the foundation for future economic prosperity.
2. NTBs have gained a more important role as instruments that can be used by governments to promote the growth and international competitiveness of specific, targeted sectors (primarily in high technology). Unlike tariffs and NTBs as applied in mature industries or in agriculture, the use of nontariff barriers as instruments of industrial and technology policies frequently is designed to manipulate the conditions under which market access is granted in order to promote transfers of technology and marketing skills to domestic firms.
3. NTBs are less constrained by international trade law than are tariffs, are more subtle in their application and potentially more restrictive than tariffs in their effect.

Although most of them do not prohibit access to markets, they act as impediments to market access and pose difficult problems for both small and large companies. They impose significant costs on firms by requiring lengthy negotiations with the governments involved and by distorting the means by which market access is achieved, if it is achieved at all. They also are frequently associated with performance requirements that are onerous and, if agreed upon, can injure the long-term market power of potential exporters.

4. Corporate decisionmakers seeking to gain access to a potentially lucrative market are unlikely to have anticipated the nature and extent of NTBs before committing their firms to the market. The legality of NTBs is often unclear and such restrictions tend to be viewed as part of the ordinary cost of doing business. The corporate decisionmaker's problem may be compounded by the dispersion of authority and plethora of government agencies in the foreign country or in Washington. Long and sometimes inconclusive negotiations will be needed to reconcile differences with foreign government agencies, often making the corporation contend with an extended period of uncertainty and a raising of the ante as negotiations proceed.
5. NTBs have greater impacts on smaller firms than on larger ones because of the lack of international investment by most small businesses, their inexperience in international trade matters, and their lack of resources to devote to responding to NTBs. This problem is critical because small firms in a rapid growth stage need an unlimited access to markets to regain the funds they have invested in new products and services as quickly as possible. It also is important since NTBs can prevent small firms with high-quality products and services from establishing themselves in markets that can make important contributions to their growth. Not being a first entrant in foreign markets can result in the loss of a significant amount of current and future business.
6. Small firms lack the resources to respond to NTBs. A small firm hoping to enter foreign markets does not have an experienced staff that is familiar with host government officials and local regulations. It often cannot commit a great amount of resources to obtaining approval for its product or service when an NTB is involved. As a result, the costs of reacting to an NTB may make it unprofitable for a smaller firm to enter a

foreign market. It may withdraw and lose sales that could have contributed to its growth because the costs of dealing with an NTB are too high. The special problems of small firms are particularly important here given their large number in high-technology industries.

7. When NTBs make it difficult to deliver a final product or establish a service network, a small U.S. firm may be forced to work through a larger U.S. company to market its product or service. This results in a loss of control and less familiarity with a foreign market. It also retards the development of important international marketing skills in the small firm. Small firms are at a disadvantage in redesigning or adapting products and services to foreign markets. The current high costs of financing foreign trade also discourage small firms from doing business in nations that have NTBs. These problems have led small firms to reduce their R&D spending for foreign markets.
8. Large multinational firms often are more successful in responding to NTBs because they have staffs and operations in many foreign markets. This can create problems for U.S. government policymakers because U.S. multinationals are prone to strike their own deals with foreign governments, thereby undercutting the efforts of our own policymakers to create an industry consensus around the elimination of specific NTBs. Indeed, there is evidence of large U.S. firms actively supporting a foreign NTB that protects its local market. The foreign nationals that work for U.S. multinationals know which parts of foreign governments must be visited in order to negotiate a way around an NTB because they have invested much time in establishing such contacts with host governments and becoming very familiar with the laws, practices and customs of the host nation.
9. High-technology industries that require high levels of investment and are easily affected by standards, licensing and government procurement are likely to have the NTBs that are most harmful to U.S. companies. At present, the telecommunications, space, and aircraft industries face the greatest difficulties with NTBs. In telecommunications, the large investments made in infrastructure by the EEC are likely to be protected by the development of standards and protocols that vary greatly from those employed in the United States.
10. NTBs often force U.S. companies to license their products in foreign countries or to enter joint ventures

with local partners. This is one way to obtain some profits from foreign sales to blocked markets. However, such a response reduces the U.S. firm's control over its foreign operations and limits its knowledge of new demands emerging in the marketplace. Direct foreign investment in a foreign country often helps to overcome an NTB and is a suitable alternative to licensing and joint ventures.

11. There is a distinct need for the U.S. government to have better information about NTBs and their impacts on individual firms and industries and on the U.S. economy. Available data sources are out of date and do not focus on the high-technology sectors that are the focus of many harmful NTBs.

POLICY RECOMMENDATIONS

1. The expertise of government agencies and offices that deal with NTBs facing U.S. high-technology firms must be increased dramatically. High-technology industries are based on increasingly complex technologies. Only with better understanding of these technologies and how NTBs can affect them will the access of U.S. firms to markets for the products of these industries be protected.
2. Definite performance criteria must be included in any arrangements that are negotiated for a reduction of NTBs. One problem with the results of recent bilateral negotiations, particularly talks to open up the Japanese telecommunications market to U.S. firms, has been the failure on the part of the Japanese to liberalize trade as rapidly as had been expected by U.S. firms. Without definite goals and timetables, U.S. firms become discouraged with the results produced by trade negotiations and are less willing to focus on the problem of NTBs. This suggests a greater sectoral focus in future bilateral and multilateral negotiations in high technology. While not entirely to be welcomed, sectoral agreements lend themselves to better monitoring and correspond more closely than do agreements by trade barrier type, to the sectoral foci of foreign government targeting efforts.
3. The U.S. Trade Representative should focus on negotiations to remove the most troublesome NTBs. This will require an in-depth focus on a few key high-technology

industries such as telecommunications, space, and aircraft. It also will require a focus on several nations most prone to use NTBs such as Japan, Korea, and France.

4. The trade agencies--particularly USTR and Commerce--should become more pro-active in the identification of NTBs. The conviction that all NTBs are either the subjects of company complaints to our government or are dealt with successfully by industry is widespread among the agencies, and probably misplaced. It ignores the small- and medium-sized firms, which seem disinclined to protest such restrictions in Washington, and frequently are incapable of circumventing restrictions abroad; and it assumes that the distortions in corporate behavior associated with private adjustments to NTBs (licensing of technology, for example) involve no public, longer-term costs.
5. The U.S. Department of Commerce should make NTBs a special focus of its industry advisory groups for high-technology sectors (ISACs). This effort should be coordinated with the Trade Representative's Office and used as a vehicle to promote government-industry cooperation, improve the exchange of information about NTBs, and help build industrial constituencies to promote trade liberalization. Particular attention should be paid to small- and medium-sized firms. These companies are least able to cope with NTBs on their own; increasingly interested in exporting; and most neglected as a source of advice, data and support to U.S. trade negotiations. USTR and Commerce should play a more active role in encouraging these firms to participate in advisory bodies and to bring their problems to the attention of the trade agencies individually.
6. The targeted use of NTBs by foreign governments to promote the growth of specific high-technology sectors should be followed carefully by USTR. This knowledge should be compiled in a systematic way and disseminated to the Congress so that institutional information about this issue is provided in a well-recorded manner. The present preference to rely on the memory of experienced individuals often leads to information gaps in government agencies.
7. An up-to-date data base on NTBs should be established by the U.S. government. It should focus on high-technology industries and include the means to track how

NTBs are often used in combination to achieve specific objectives.

8. Special attention should be paid by U.S. policymakers to the use of incompatible standards and protocols by foreign governments in industries such as telecommunications. A negotiating initiative should be undertaken by USTR before this problem becomes insoluble.
9. An early-warning mechanism should be established within the Commerce Department or Trade Representative's Office to provide industry with rapid information about changes in foreign governments' use of NTBs.
10. Another focus of negotiations should be those NTBs that are imposed on U.S. companies but not their indigenous counterparts in foreign markets, such as the need to do testing to meet acceptance criteria in the United States, rather than in the host country.
11. A long-range strategy for negotiations to remove NTBs should be developed by USTR. This should give NTBs more of a professional emphasis and underscore the long-term goals of trade liberalization and their benefits for U.S. firms.

1
Introduction

THE IMPORTANCE OF NONTARIFF BARRIERS

Nontariff barriers (NTBs) have gained increasing prominence (relative to tariffs) as impediments to market access. They pose difficult problems for both small and large companies. These barriers are less constrained by international trade law than are tariffs, are more subtle in their application and potentially more restrictive than tariffs in their effect. Although most of them do not prohibit access to markets, they impose significant costs on firms by requiring lengthy negotiations with the governments involved. They frequently are associated with performance requirements that are onerous and, which, if agreed upon, can injure the long-term market power of potential exporters.

NTBs present great problems for small firms, which often cannot sustain the costs of extended negotiations, are more jeopardized by performance requirements (for technology transfers, for example) and have less political clout within the trade agencies in Washington. As a consequence, they are more likely than larger firms to abandon the protected market entirely. Large firms can use their experience as multinationals to overcome many NTBs in host nations, but they can still face important barriers to significant markets.

If U.S. firms in high-technology sectors are to succeed in the international marketplace, the government and those firms must learn more about the barriers that are particularly vexing for such firms. They also must know more about the markets and sectors that are the focus of barriers, and the strategies that can be adopted to circumvent or mitigate their effects.

Two phenomena that have grown in importance in recent years prompted this study. The first is the proliferation of NTBs adopted by foreign governments, especially those of the developed nations. The lessening of tariff levels flowing from the Kennedy and Tokyo rounds of trade negotiations has resulted in the increased prominence of NTBs as the primary instrument of import market protection (as well as export subsidization). The second phenomenon is the increased volume, range, and importance of technology-related decisions by U.S. firms. These decisions include those relating to budgeting and siting of research and development (R&D) activity; protecting and commercializing innovations; developing and adapting products for introduction into foreign markets; and relative emphasis on exporting versus licensing versus foreign direct investment as a vehicle for technology and product diffusion. More generally, these decisions relate to the host of factors falling under the rubric of technology transfer.

It was our belief that these two phenomena were not independent and that NTBs influence the technology-related behavior of U.S. firms. The causal link is undoubtedly reciprocal--that is, behavior by U.S. firms affects the types/volume of NTBs adopted by foreign governments. In addition, the two phenomena are not isolated ones and instead touch on a wide variety of policy areas (trade, technology, national security, etc.) that can be influenced by U.S. government policy.

The belief that NTBs influence the technology-related behavior of U.S. firms flows from a number of facts. First, these NTBs (which are generally barriers to trade but occasionally act as incentives to trade--e.g., export subsidies) frequently have a high technology orientation. The actual form of the NTBs--standards and specifications, degree of patent protection, licensing requirements, government procurement of goods and services (including funding of R&D), etc.--tends to embrace products and services that are technology intensive. Protectionist impulses (in response to stagnant growth and high unemployment throughout the developed world) have resulted in NTBs that protect fledgling high-technology industries or preserve the labor intensiveness (and, thus, the employment levels) of traditional industries.

Second, previous research had demonstrated that trade restrictions (in general) have a pronounced effect on company behavior and especially on export and investment strategies. Traditional product cycle models traced the way to exploit comparative advantage and maintain a technology lead: a progression from exporting from home to investing and producing abroad to licensing foreign firms to use the mature, older technology.[1] Government policy in the form of NTBs can distort this process, creating barriers to entry of the foreign competition. These barriers and policies can influence a firm's decision on whether and how to enter a foreign market, whether to accept technology-transfer requirements as preconditions to market access, and whether to introduce the original product or adapt it to local needs/preferences. In such cases, nontariff barriers are instruments of industrial and technology policies, used less to exclude access to the market than to manipulate the conditions under which market access is granted in order to promote transfers of technology and marketing skills to domestic firms.

Superimposed on these goals of industrial promotion have been the secular decline of mature industries in the developed countries, which has stimulated protectionist pressures and the imposition of conventional nontariff barriers to ease the adjustment burden (or to prevent adjustment); and by cyclical factors that, in their recent severity, have led to a--hopefully--temporary increase in protectionism. Finally, there is the fact that our definition of what constitutes a trade barrier has expanded through the Tokyo Round negotiations and subsequent ministerial conferences and bilateral discussions to encompass policy measures heretofore defined as domestic.

PROJECT TASKS

This research was conducted in four phases: project definition, surveys and interviews, NTB evaluation and policy implications, and analysis of the short-term future and reporting of results.

In the project definition phase, we had planned to produce a compendium of NTBs to be used in subsequent research phases--for example, developing a set of testable hypotheses, collecting background data on the relevant NTBs and nations, etc. This task proved to be extremely difficult because of the poor coverage of NTBs in high-technology industries in existing data bases. Although a number of sources were explored (see Appendix A for a more complete discussion of this problem), we pressed on with case studies of specific sectors and an analysis of types of NTBs.

In the second phase, we developed a set of specific and testable hypotheses for use in our interviews. This task was founded on a careful search of the relevant literature on industrial organization and international economics and on the insights of study team members, but depended primarily on interviews with individuals from high-technology firms. A number of preliminary hypotheses were evaluated. These include:

1. NTBs are closely linked to national industrial goals. Particularly in industries selected for their strategic importance to national growth by individual nations,

NTBs are likely to be employed in order to limit competition in areas defined as crucial to national economic security. As a consequence, products requiring a sizeable amount of R&D and marketing are likely to be affected.

2. A goal of NTBs is to isolate individual national markets from the world market so that foreign companies with production advantages that depend on economies of scale, worldwide marketing programs, and worldwide financial sourcing cannot exploit these advantages in the local market that is small and specialized. This runs counter to American trade policy, which argues for open access to all markets on an equal footing.
3. If NTBs block entry into particular markets, R&D priorities in firms are shifted to emphasize existing markets, although this may result in a decline in long-range competition of U.S. firms in the markets they are unable to enter.
4. NTBs sometimes are used to promote licensing of new products by U.S. firms. While many U.S. high-technology companies have been willing to do this in the past, some are recognizing the loss of control over product development and market information that results from licensing, and are resorting to joint ventures with foreign companies or foreign direct investment to avoid outright licensing.
5. NTBs, by making access to foreign markets more difficult, historically have led U.S. high-technology firms to establish local operations abroad and to develop close ties with the agencies regulating their products. As local facilities have become costlier to support and market entry has required greater efforts, foreign direct investment has become a less-preferred choice. Instead, arrangements with governments, with competitors and joint-venture partners have been employed as a means to obtain market access.
6. As a result of the close ties forged with local regulating agencies, American companies normally are inclined to negotiate the condition of their market access directly with the local government. Such an arrangement is convenient as it generally is based on a preestablished relationship with the government, and is reasonably secure as the government both sets and monitors the terms of the agreement. U.S. trade officials often learn of such agreements after they have gone into effect, if at all.

7. Large companies familiar with the intricacies of foreign markets generally will not come to the government for assistance in penetrating foreign markets. Because of the large number of jobs and size of the investment that these firms could generate, they normally prefer to negotiate their own conditions of market access with the host government. Small companies, however, would be more likely to come to U.S. trade offices for assistance in penetrating barriers, were they more aware of their rights under international trade law. However, these firms generally are new-to-export and are unfamiliar with the regulations and requirements they face. Oftentimes, although the degree is uncertain, these firms will not even make the attempt to export because of the regulatory complexities involved.

In the third phase, we chose NTBs for intensive analysis, concentrating on foreign markets including the United Kingdom, France, West Germany and Japan. These markets are both large and well integrated, meaning that the effects of NTBs will be discernible more readily. The choice of industries was based both on our evaluation of NTBs (choosing sectors where NTBs are concentrated) and on our conviction that NTBs in high-technology sectors pose special problems for firms and U.S. trade policy officials distinct from those associated with mature sectors.

In this phase, we used structured and open-ended questions to explore the following topics:

- Target and scope of NTBs. We started with questions on this topic to ensure that our preliminary results from Phase I on the target and scope of NTBs are correct.
- R&D structure. For both the respondent's company and the industry as a whole, we wanted to obtain information on the level, location, and source of funding for R&D.
- Purpose of foreign R&D. Is the primary function of foreign R&D to develop/modify products and services for a foreign market? To do basic research for the parent company? To fulfill local content or technology transfer regulations? To develop products for both U.S. and foreign markets?
- Associated topics. How does national government targeting of key industries affect NTBs?
- Policy questions. How do U.S. and foreign national security, trade, and technology policies alter the picture? What pending changes might change the link

and in what ways? What is expected to happen in the short-term future?

ORGANIZATION OF FINAL REPORT

Contents of the final report include:

- An executive summary reporting key results
- An introduction to NTBs
- Background on the types of NTBs
- An analysis of the impacts of NTBs
- An analysis of the impact of NTBs on corporate decision-making
- An analysis of the impact of NTBs on U.S. policy
- A discussion of conclusions and policy recommendations.

In addition, appendixes to the report contain panel and interview results, and a review of the currently available data bases on NTBs.

NOTES

1. Raymond Vernon has added an important twist by noting how the generation of new technology by foreign R&D units can supplement the diffusion of older technology to exploit the last vestige of comparative advantage.

2 Nontariff Barriers and High-Technology Trade

NONTARIFF BARRIERS AND THE PROMOTION OF HIGH-TECHNOLOGY INDUSTRIES

Traditional Uses and New High-Technology Focus

Nontariff barriers have been in existence for some time, primarily as a means to limit market entry in order to protect infant industries. A study by the International Trade Commission in the early 1970s[1] described the range of NTBs in use and underscored their preeminent role in protecting industries in their infancy in nations where they were employed. Today, however, there is a further trend toward targeting NTBs to promote specific national development goals in high-technology industries. Such barriers are intended less to prohibit market access than to manipulate the conditions under which access takes place. Thus, a number of NTBs in use in developed and developing nations have been enacted largely to obtain new technology and know-how. Better access to these factors is expected to promote the growth of high-technology industries, thus serving the interest of national development goals.

Traditionally, NTBs have protected infant industries in consumer durables, capital goods, and other mature sectors. In these sectors, NTBs have provided protective barriers as the utility of tariff protection was reduced by a series of multilateral agreements. Through administrative procedures, such as customs regulations, safety standards and health regulations, nations have prohibited products from entering markets they want to reserve for national firms. An excellent example of this type of protection is RCA's attempt to market color TVs in France. The French TV system requires a different tube design than that employed in nearly all other nations. Although RCA developed a TV tube that was suitable for sale in France, standards for the emission of radiation from the rear of the TV were used to block RCA's entry into the French market. By excluding RCA from the French market, the French government assured its national firms of a dominance over the internal market. Since they could sell only in France, this protection was essential to the survival of the indigenous industry.[2] However, this protection provided little stimulus for increased R&D spending, the development of products suitable for export, or greater foreign investment. On the contrary, the use of NTBs as barriers to competition probably isolated firms from technological advances and made them more risk-averse.[3]

A very different range of objectives encourages the enactment of NTBs for development purposes. In these cases, NTBs are established by nations to gain greater access to new technologies and know-how. The final result that countries hope to achieve is the improvement of the technological status of national firms. NTBs are used to promote increased R&D spending, to facilitate the development of competitive exports, and to promote foreign investment by high-technology companies. A good illustration of development-oriented NTBs is the case of copyright legislation for software in Japan. The Ministry of International Trade and Industry (MITI) proposed that there be a fifteen-year statute of limitations on software copyrights in Japan[4] and that any company selling software in Japan be required to divulge the code containing the basic program necessary to design the package. If U.S. companies had to conform to the latter proposal, their Japanese competitors would obtain access to critical information that would enhance their ability to write more sophisticated software. Such information also would facilitate the jump to fifth-generation software that the Japanese believe is the centerpiece required for the development of supercomputers and high-speed applications programs for business.[5]

This promotion of targeted national industries can create problems for policymakers in a world dominated by multinational firms. Targeting a single industry for growth by improving domestic technological status may force firms to break traditional patterns of sourcing and reduce their ability to operate as multinationals. For example, multinational electronics companies are often asked or forced to buy semiconductors from domestic sources although they have cheaper and well-established foreign sources, as has been the case in France and Germany. In these cases, targeting with NTBs can reduce the funds that multinationals, both domestic and foreign, have available to promote foreign expansion and to devote to new R&D. Some nations also attempt to keep foreign multinationals from licensing new technologies developed as a result of domestic research programs, that is, the Japanese VLSI programs. Because of such barriers, foreign multinationals may be reluctant to increase host nation investment and to transfer technology to local affiliates so they can exploit the new technologies.

Development-oriented NTBs intended to promote national firms can severely limit the operations of domestic multinationals with well-developed systems for sourcing and gaining access to overseas R&D. Other NTBs can work in a perverse manner to discourage the entry of foreign multinationals when nations hope NTBs will improve the technology available to national firms. NTBs may therefore limit the introduction of new technology and new investment into a host nation's economy rather than promote it.

Types of Nontariff Barriers

There are several general categories of NTBs that are used to promote high-technology industries. These include (1) regulatory policies, (2) bureaucratic barriers, and (3) private-sector limitations. Regulatory policies include licensing, standards of all types (both testing and certification), antitrust laws, financial market regulation (for banks, securities firms and other financial intermediaries), and investment regulations (performance requirements and offset and coproduction agreements). Performance requirements are used by governments to compel multinational firms to agree that incoming investments, R&D, and technology will help achieve a host nation's objectives for a targeted industry. They may require the export of a certain quantity of a product, the use of a specified amount of local inputs, or the offsetting of the multinational's imports by its exports.[6] Offset and coproduction agreements require a foreign firm to enter into a subcontracting arrangement, license production, agree to buy certain amounts of goods from civilian or defense producers, or enter into arrangements to produce high-technology products with a local firm. In some cases, guarantees to purchase goods and services from the buyer country, which are a condition of the offset agreement, lead to large transfers of R&D and countertrade.

Bureaucratic barriers can include customs practices, especially customs valuations, quotas, government procurement agreements, and administrative guidance. Barriers to trade in services, especially transborder data flows, result in situations where crucial information about design and production techniques, about know-how, and about strategies for marketing high-technology products cannot be accessed from a foreign market but must be kept in local facilities. This can help improve the technology available to targeted industries in local markets.

Private-sector limitations include restrictions on distribution systems. These have been criticized as one of the main means by which access of American firms to Japan's markets is restricted. These barriers are not governmental, but are the consequence of the Japanese system of marketing and close relationships between Japanese marketers and the corporations they serve.

A number of these barriers have more of an impact on high-technology industries than on other sectors. In the section that follows, the purposes of NTBs are discussed in greater detail to demonstrate how they influence high-technology sectors.

PURPOSES OF NTBs IN HIGH TECHNOLOGY

The Pursuit of National Development Goals

The case of copyrights on software discussed above illustrates the development goals that nations hope to achieve by imposing NTBs on high-technology products. Countries expect to gain greater access to the know-how that firms in high-technology industries require to improve their products and processes. By forcing more sophisticated firms to agree to licensing and to coproduction or offset agreements, governments hope to gain detailed information about new technologies for domestic companies. Rather than barring access to their markets, nations want foreign high-technology firms to enter them. But, by using NTBs, countries want to place conditions on this entry. Thus, governments use NTBs in a way that not only challenges national firms to become more competitive, but also provides better access to advanced technologies that national firms need to compete.

Such NTBs are intended to boost R&D spending by national firms, to increase exports of high-technology goods, and to promote foreign direct investment by national high-technology companies. Once national firms become more familiar with new technologies, they lessen the risk involved in creating new products and processes.[7] They can then become greater risk-takers and develop advantages in the marketplace that differentiate them from their rivals. If successful in exploiting such advantages, national firms can expand the edge they have over their rivals and create a technology gap, enabling them to overtake foreign rivals that once dominated the markets in which they compete.[8]

The Japanese government's strategy of blocking Texas Instruments' entry into Japan's markets is a good example of this use of targeted NTBs. Structural factors limited Texas Instruments' development of a distribution network, and NTBs were used to restrict its share of the emerging local market until the firm agreed to license some of its technology. As a result, Japan gained access to know-how and design technology to spur the growth of a competitive national semiconductor industry.[9] This licensing restriction appears to have resulted in greater Japanese R&D spending, a refocusing of R&D funds on products with a greater profit potential, an improvement in export sales and an enhancement of the foreign investment potential of national firms.

In another case, the French are seriously considering the enactment of further barriers to transborder data flows as a means to improve the status of the high-technology work that takes place in France. By limiting the ability of foreign multinational firms that operate in France to use international communications, the French hope to gain access to recent research and new technologies. This could occur since restrictions on transborder data flows would force more investment in these types of operations locally. This use of NTBs also is very different from previous ones; rather than acting to block the inflow of products, it would restrict both inflows and outflows. Such a policy will force companies wishing to do business in France to develop and store more know-how locally.[10] In addition, keeping this information in domestic facilities will give France the ability to regulate its use.

Potential Impacts on Technology Decisions of U.S. Firms

The use of NTBs by foreign governments to target specific high-technology industries for gains in competitiveness can lead to a reorientation of U.S. companies' R&D decisions, foreign investment plans, export promotion programs and the volume and allocation of R&D spending. U.S. companies' R&D decisions can be changed if NTBs are used to target specific foreign industries. Their inability to compete in some markets because of exclusionary standards, licensing procedures, coproduction arrangements and government procurement policies can reduce the returns to R&D from products that face targeting. If returns are lower than expected, R&D funding can be reduced or R&D funds may be shifted into other areas where profits are greater and the risk of facing NTBs is lower. The need to license know-how in order to enter foreign markets lessens the control that U.S. firms have over new technologies. If this lowers returns to R&D efforts, firms may reduce R&D spending or shift R&D to other sectors.

If NTBs limit the position of U.S. high-technology products in foreign markets, U.S. firms may become much more reluctant to invest abroad. NTBs that reduce the flow of information and the ability of U.S. firms to manage a far-flung network of operations can have the same results. Barriers to transborder data flow also can have this impact. In one case, Motorola expressed its concern that French and German restrictions could force it to establish "expensive data processing facilities in each country duplicating already existing facilities" and to locate product test facilities and engineering design centers in those nations that restrict the shipment of test, certification and design data. NCR and Xerox also have raised similar concerns because restrictions on data flows would increase their cost of doing business in Europe.[11]

NTBs also affect export promotion programs for high-technology firms. If standards and other NTBs act to bar market entry, American firms' exports can decline. On the other hand, if foreign investments are blocked, exports may become a substitute for producing high-technology goods abroad. This can occur if licensing requirements, coproduction or joint production agreements in host nations limit the ability of U.S. companies to produce abroad. Other considerations may also lead U.S. firms to emphasize exports over foreign direct investment. These could include the loss of control over critical know-how that would result from complying with licensing and coproduction requirements.

CONDITIONS THAT AFFECT SUCCESS OR FAILURE OF NTBs

A number of factors often are considered crucial in the success of NTBs. These include: the oligopolistic role of firms in the high-technology sector; the timing of state intervention and the possibility of early innovators achieving significant advantages in global markets; differences among nations and firms in the state of technology; and the ability to achieve economies of scale through increased vertical integration. Each of these will be discussed here.

As Knickerbocker has shown, oligopolistic firms achieve innovative advances over their rivals that can be protected over sizeable periods in the product life cycle.[12] If such advantages can be made cumulative, it is logical to use NTBs to protect the development of oligopolists. But this is true only if oligopolistic firms can exploit these new advantages, gained through heavier R&D concentration on important areas for emerging products, better than nonoligopolistic firms. This may have been the case in a sector such as autos, where NTBs set up by Japan to protect local markets facilitated important R&D-based innovations in design and production that resulted in a large cost advantage.

A different way to reach the same goal is where one government is more prescient than others. If one government supports early and significant innovations, it can substantially alter a firm's or an industry's position in global markets. Government procurement thus has been utilized to promote a rapid expansion in R&D spending in an emerging sector. Good illustrations of this are the sizeable role played by NTT procurement in supporting Japanese telecommunications development and by the French Post, Telephone, and Telegraph (PTT) Administration in promoting French digital communications development. In each case, the use of government procurement to promote these areas was not responded to by rival governments until very recently, although it led to the isolation of domestic markets from foreign competition. Some officials in the Department of Commerce have argued that this was a consequence of the poor bargaining position of the U.S. government.[13] The lag in response time may have been crucial, since it gave the French sufficient time to focus additional R&D on specific breakthroughs in order to provide domestic firms with advantages over their rivals in world markets. Latecomers may now face large barriers to entry in the fields that have been supported by government policies in these nations and in world markets.

Differences in the existing state of technology in a specific sector also may make the imposition of NTBs attractive. In such a situation, using NTBs may enable governments to provide leading firms with a way to begin to accumulate an innovative edge over foreign rivals. This advantage can be increased if access to the technology is difficult, or if differential levels of profitability can be maintained by exploiting this innovative edge in world markets. If this is possible, an industry or firm would be able to differentiate itself from its rivals in other nations over a period of years. The laggards' ability to catch up may be impeded if they face special situations. One might be where the processes involved in innovation could not be replicated easily by copying because they depended upon achieving certain critical advances in technology that were built upon a series of cumulative steps. Another might occur if the key processes were based on the development of advantages in process engineering that depended upon a build-up of skills in technical work forces that took time to replicate.

Vertical integration may provide the proper conditions to exploit NTBs in high-technology industries. Extra R&D spending can be focused on critical processes or products if additional funds can be obtained from the use of NTBs. This extra allocation of R&D to specific products may be exploited more readily by vertically integrated firms since they can achieve cost advantages in crucial intermediate products used in the final goods they produce. As a result, extra R&D spending may provide these vertically integrated firms with a key competitive edge over their rivals. One would expect that such advantages could be eroded once the new technology is understood. However, if they involved major advances in technology or an accumulation of innovative improvements in processes, it might take considerable time for rivals to close the existing gap. This strategy may be at the heart of the success of Japanese auto and computer firms.

Vertical integration also may be important if NTBs permit firms to export more quickly than they had expected to. In such a case, the economies achieved through vertical integration could be exploited to an even greater degree as the result of increased exports (and a growth in domestic production). This may even be a prime motivating factor since NTBs added to conditions that distort free market competition may result in large improvements in competitive status.

There is a strong desire on the part of governments to use NTBs to help their firms leapfrog ahead of competitors in high-technology industries. By limiting market entry and enabling national corporations to raise their prices in the domestic market due to a lack of competition, governments provide national corporations with a subsidy similar to that gained by firms in agriculture or in more mature industries when tariffs or nontariff barriers are used. These measures also can have an inputed positive impact. The extra profits gained as a consequence of NTBs in the case of high-technology industries can facilitate increases in R&D spending and enable protected firms to be more risk-prone in their allocation of R&D funds. Sizeable improvements in competitiveness can be gained from prolonged increases in R&D spending and from innovation in areas that more risk-averse firms fail to explore. Domestic firms can become more aggressive in their high-technology product export strategies, in their foreign direct investment behavior and in their licensing of technology. This assumes, however, that most production is primarily national (a case that may hold in some sectors such as biotechnology and flexible manufacturing) and that market responses by other governments do not reduce the benefits gained by the nations blocking access to their own domestic markets through the use of nontariff barriers.

In summary, NTBs often are used to encourage host nation firms to catch up and overtake their rivals. Many developed and developing nations have visions of repeating the Japanese experience in autos and believe that NTBs are a critical tool required to achieve rapid industrial growth. By permitting substantial improvements in technology and competitiveness through the imposition of NTBs--often in concert with promotional programs for R&D, exports, and training--governments expect their high-technology firms to mimic Japan's. Whether these expectations are realistic is uncertain, since the influence of NTBs on R&D allocation and decisions, and on firm behavior related to new technologies, is not well understood. The subsequent tasks in this project will explore the impact of NTBs on corporate technology decisions in greater detail. The following chapter will focus on specific types of NTBs, how they are used and potential consequences for the involved firms.

NOTES

1. U.S. Tariff Commission, Non-Tariff Trade Barriers, a report to the U.S. Senate, Committee on Finance (Washington, D.C.: U.S. Government Printing Office, 1974).

2. Interview with Donald R. Bronson, President, Federated Technology and Electronics Corporation, New York, a former employee of RCA-France.

3. Frank H. Knight, Risk, Uncertainty and Profit (New York: Harper & Row, 1965).

4. This is much less than the fifty-year limit now set by the World Intellectual Property Organization. However, this part of the proposal is far less important than the proposal that software codes be disclosed.

5. Discussion with Lloyd Kaufman, Senior Advisor, Charles L. Fishman, P.C., Washington, D.C., formerly research director with CBEEMA, the trade association of the 45 largest computer manufacturers in the United States. While this proposal by MITI was withdrawn from consideration by the Japanese Diet during 1984, it is very likely to be resubmitted in 1985. In addition, the proposed policy parallels policies already enforced by Brazil. For a discussion of these policies and their impact on foreign manufacturers' presence in the Brazilian market, see United Nations, Centre on Transnational Corporations, Transborder Data Flows and Brazil: A Case Study (New York: United Nations, 1983). South Korea and Canada are other nations that have been extremely interested in the Brazilian experience. There are some

indications that they will begin to restrict the sale of software in the near future. Both nations have been active participants in the debate over transborder data flows and have implemented policies to force computer service firms to do more data processing within their borders rather than in foreign installations. This debate has become extremely political in nature over the last few years; see the discussion in Joan Spero, "Information: The Policy Void," Foreign Policy, No. 48 (Fall 1982), pp. 139-156.

6. The Labor Industry Coalition for International Trade, Performance Requirements (Washington, D.C.: LICIT, 1981).

7. Knight, Risk, Uncertainty and Profit, Chs. 5 and 6.

8. U.S. Department of Commerce, International Trade Administration, The Computer Industry, April 1983.

9. Discussion with Charles Mathey, The Futures Group, formerly Manager of Multinational Strategic Planning, Motorola.

10. Discussions with Lloyd Kaufman, Senior Advisor; Charles L. Fishman, P.C., Washington, D.C.; and Joseph Zycherman, International Policy Advisor, AT&T Information Systems, Morristown, New Jersey.

11. U.S., Congress, House, Committee on Government Operations, Subcommittee on Government Information and Individual Rights, International Data Flow (Washington, D.C.: U.S. Government Printing Office, 1980), pp. 653, 650, and 782- 764.

12. Frederick Knickerbocker, Oligopolistic Reaction and Multinational Enterprise (Boston, Mass.: Graduate School of Business Administration, Harvard University, 1973).

13. U.S., Congress, Senate, Committee on Commerce, Science and Transportation, Long-Range Goals in International Telecommunications and Information: An Outline for United States Policy, prepared by the U.S. Department of Commerce, National Telecommunications and Information Administration (Washington, D.C.: U.S. Government Printing Office, 1983), pp. 161-162.

3
The Classification of NTBs: Some Illustrations of Impacts

STANDARDS

Definition

Technical barriers to trade are among the most common of nontariff barriers. The wide range of concerns they address, ranging from health and safety to product quality to protection of the home market, has fostered a plethora of standards taking a variety of forms. In recent years, standards issues have taken on increased importance in world trade as the rate of technological change has quickened. In some industries, such as telecommunications or computers, the pace of product development has exceeded the ability of major trading partners to establish commonly accepted standards. This has created a chaotic situation where national technical requirements have become obstacles to trade. Trade in some advanced sectors has suffered from deliberately discriminatory national standards designed principally for the protection and development of domestic industries.[1]

The difficulties involved in distinguishing the illegitimate barriers from the legitimate have made standards a contentious issue. Most standards do address legitimate nontrade issues; likewise, most have an effect on trade.[2] The debate turns on the purportedly unintended side effects, and on whether less-trade-restricting measures exist to achieve the express intent (protection of health and safety, promotion of innovation, etc.).

The existence of these differing and trade-restricting standards has curtailed market access for foreign firms, and dissuaded some from even making the attempt. American firms certainly have found the transition to export more difficult because of the inconsistent international array of technical requirements. American manufacturers are not always inclined similarly to use international norms for their own standards, and thus contribute to the confusion they face in world markets. This problem is exacerbated for established technologies, such as data processing, which are not regulated by a commonly accepted international system of standards. There is a critical need for accepted operating norms in these industries, yet just whose norms are to be applied is a difficulty that, up to now, has remained unsolved. American manufacturers in the computer and telecommunications industries, for example, allege that European representatives to international standards-setting meetings hold more influence over the outcome than does the American representative. Moreover, the International Standards Organization (ISO) on average requires five years to develop a standard. Seen in this light, today's rapidly developing industries cannot, by definition, have agreed-upon standards.[3]

In examining firms' responses to standards-related NTBs, it is noteworthy that these barriers are used by manufacturers to secure a competitive advantage over rivals. Each company responds differently. Some firms are well connected in their markets and can anticipate or influence changes in standards far better than their competitors. Others are simply more persistent. In 1979, the ROLM Corporation attempted to market a digital PBX in Japan only to find that NTT did not yet have standards for a fully digital system. Undeterred, ROLM set up a staff in Tokyo and worked with NTT to develop the technical specifications which, of course, were suited to ROLM's product. At the same time GTE attempted to market its digital system in Japan. Yet, finding no standards to certify and approve its product, GTE turned to Washington and complained. ROLM succeeded; GTE did not. The responses, and marketing successes, of these firms could hardly have been more divergent.[4]

The Standards Code

The importance of standards, testing, and certification requirements in international trade was, until recent years, not fully appreciated. In part because of the complexity of the issue, and the more obvious need for a reduction in tariff levels, standards received virtually no attention in the GATT or other multilateral bodies until the mid-1960s. After the Kennedy Round early in the decade (which succeeded in reducing nonagricultural tariffs by an average 35 percent), attention to a large degree shifted to nontariff issues. First addressed in the GATT in 1967, the negotiations were transferred to the broader forum of the Tokyo Round of Multilateral Trade Negotiations in 1975. Standards as an issue at the Tokyo Round were emphasized by the U.S.

delegation primarily as a result of its experience with the (then) Tripartite Accord, a UK-French-FRG draft agreement to develop European technical specifications in electronics that would challenge U.S military specifications. In the early 1970s, the Electronics Industry Association launched a major campaign on this issue, claiming a potential trade loss of $200 million annually.

The Agreement on Technical Barriers to Trade (the Standards Code) finally entered into force on January 1, 1980, as one of the six "Codes" of the Tokyo Round.[5] The complexity of the subject is reflected in the framing of the Code. It recognizes standards as an important and necessary expression of national sovereignty, and seeks to ensure that standard and certification systems are not used as intentional barriers to trade. Imports are to receive treatment no less favorable than that accorded to locally produced products.[6] No particular standard is proscribed, nor is an attempt made to identify specific, discriminatory practices, given the huge array of technical standards. Instead, the Code establishes rules under which standards and certification programs are prepared, adopted, and applied, and by which products are tested for conformity.

The Code's requirements and provisions are thorough.[7] Yet the amorphous nature of the issue would, the framers recognized, make enforcement difficult (despite the inclusion of dispute settlement provisions), and the Committee on Technical Barriers to Trade was established to deal with this anticipated problem. A further concern was that, with the exception of the United States, most countries had closed standards-setting systems that now had to be opened and made accessible to outsiders (transparency). Given the national bureaucratic aversion to change and, more importantly, the sensitive issue of sovereignty, the Standards Code should be viewed as a first step toward the reduction of technical barriers. It provides a means, a forum for discussion, but as the following section suggests, the end remains elusive.

Overview

Given the wide range of concerns that standards address, it is not surprising to find they take a variety of forms. As barriers to trade, the scope becomes still larger, for the availability of information regarding these standards can be an important barrier in itself. As noted above, most standards stem, at least in part, from nontrade concerns, and the difficulty lies in distinguishing the legitimate controls from the illegitimate. Some, of course, are simply nationalistic attempts to curb imports, particularly in the high-technology industries. These discriminatory standards generally are not imposed upon the high-technology content of a particular product, but rather affect the packaging and peripherals essential to the marketing of the product. In analyzing these types of barriers, it is significant that those standards foreign producers find most restrictive can often be grouped by industry, if not by country.

For example, it is interesting that, given America's inability to significantly penetrate most high-technology markets in Japan, the standards-related complaints of American exporters fall into two categories. First, there is the Japanese government's lack of transparency in setting standards and compliance regulations. Information regarding proposed, and even effected, changes in Japanese technical requirements for imports is often difficult to obtain. Second, certification has been prohibitively costly at times, or has involved delays that enabled Japanese firms to more effectively bring competitive products to market. Similarly, a common thread running through the complaints of exporters to Europe has been the restrictive level of testing and certification requirements. This has resulted not only in higher costs, but also in significant performance disadvantages for foreign-produced products vis-a-vis locally produced ones.

Testing and Certification Requirements: Case Studies

Such requirements usually stem from legitimate, nontrade concerns, yet frequently entail added costs, delays, and even exclusion from the market. Much of the difficulty here stems from a country's refusal to accept foreign test data. This has been particularly damaging to American exports in pharmaceuticals and medical electronics to Japan.[8] Long and expensive delays are involved, as complete lot samples of drugs or three sets of the electronics equipment must be submitted for testing. More generally, as foreigners (including Americans) are not allowed to self-certify, they must submit to lot inspection systems. Extensive testing backlogs for all product groups are tolerated, with the result that American exporters in all industries can expect months of delays (up to two years, in some cases). By comparison, Underwriters Laboratories (UL, the American testing/certification body) maintains an office in Japan with Japanese-speaking personnel for testing/approval of Japanese products exported to America.[9]

Refusal to accept foreign test data for certification purposes is not confined to the sensitive pharmaceutical and medical electronics industries. West Germany, generally known for its free trade stance, has developed standards for the computer industry that act as effective de facto barriers. The German Society of Engineers (VDE) has developed rigorous standards in these industries (enforced by the German PTT) that have ensured high quality in, and interchangeability among, products. Yet, the FRG does not allow self-certifications, as does the United States, and requires that VDE engineers perform the testing. Hence, American manufacturers who wish to export to Germany are normally obligated to incur the added expense of bringing VDE engineers to the United States to essentially duplicate tests already completed. The American computer manufacturer, Sperry, has complained of significantly higher costs from this NTB. Moreover, American manufacturers here must use VDE-approved components--components that often are neither produced nor marketed in the United States (because of the cost of bringing VDE engineers to America to approve them and the limited size of the U.S. market). Finally, American producers of office and photographic equipment have complained of the lengthy certification periods necessary to gain approval. The interval between submission and approval in Germany is often twice that required in the United States.[10]

Even after certification has been granted, imports may be curbed by testing procedures. Under the Japanese Electrical Appliances and Material Control Law, for example, an exporter cannot apply directly to the government for product approval, but must instead submit an application through a Japanese agent. This tightens distributors' control over American suppliers, and increases the time necessary to win approval. Even more restrictive is that after approval has been granted, any changes or improvements in product design necessitate resubmission for product testing and approval, and entail new delays. While most established American manufacturers affected by these regulations are large, and normally have subsidiaries operating in Japan to assist in gaining approval, new companies in developing fields are at a disadvantage. Innovating firms in the rapidly changing field of biotechnology, for example, normally are neither large nor have Japanese subsidiaries. Each must instead rely on an agent in Japan who holds the import license--to switch agents a firm must reapply for a new license. The delays resulting from these restrictions assist Japanese manufacturers in marketing their own competitive products.[11]

Difficulties in obtaining certification also can be found in voluntary arrangements. Japanese Industrial Standards (JIS) are entirely voluntary (except for a few isolated cases), and in 1982 covered 7,852 products (including virtually all products in the high-tech industries). The JIS marking is generally accepted as characterizing those goods of superior quality and is an advantage for sales. Yet as of 1982, fewer than one-third of the standards were available in English translation. Moreover, until very recently it was impossible for foreign products to qualify at all for the marking (no testing arrangements existed). As a result, as of April 30, 1982, there were 16,182 producers whose products qualified for the JIS marking, of which only 18 were held by non-Japanese manufacturers. The salience of this barrier is heightened by Tokyo's policy that:

> In compliance to the purport of Article 26 (Respect for Japanese Industrial Standards) of the Industrial Standardization Law, both government and public offices are recommended to give priority to the application of JIS in regard to the procurement of commodities for their own usage.[12]

Although the government has promised action on this front (in part because it is not compatible with the equal-access clause (Article 7.2) of the Standards Code), observers doubt that much change will soon be seen. Moreover, the JIS marking is granted only after a detailed inspection of the manufacturer's factory. Most American producers are naturally reluctant to allow a foreign government (i.e., competitors) access to their production processes, particularly in the high-technology industries.

Technical Standards: Case Studies

A second standards-related problem, and one even more intractable than testing and certification difficulties, lies in the technical operating requirements themselves. The West German machine tool industry is a case in point. The DIN standard is viewed by non-German producers as excessively stringent, and is a de facto technical barrier to machine tool imports as it normally requires modification of non-German products. Yet the stringency of the standard within Germany has led to a technically well-defined and high-quality product that can easily be exported as it generally satisfies less-exacting foreign standards.

Similarly, market penetration also can be hindered by a lack of standards. Product lines that have not been sufficiently defined by the international market, including most information equipment, are not manufactured according to any one set standard. Rather a variety of standards are advanced at the firm level. These differing technical operating requirements effectively prevent computers and word processors from interfacing with different makes on-site, let alone overseas. Export markets are segmented as purchasers opt for systems compatible with their installed base. The market dominance of market leaders, such as IBM or Xerox, is thereby maintained to the detriment of smaller producers. These smaller producers, moreover, are often uncertain which standards to use in their own production. Standards for local area networks, for example, are presently being advanced by IBM, Xerox, the European Computer Manufacturers' Association, and the Institute of Electrical and Electronic Engineers in the United States. The U.K. Department of Industry, sensing both user and manufacturer frustration, has attempted to remedy this by identifying and promoting emerging standards without waiting for their formal publication. Unfortunately this intercept system appears to have little chance for success.[13]

Standards at the national level are often more discriminatory. The French color television industry, for example, has developed behind the protective national SECAM standard. This has helped Thomson-CSF hold its own share of the market in France, but has not led to significant market penetration abroad.[14] In Britain, the Department of Industry has pressured British Telecom (BT) for an approvals scheme for telephone equipment that would allow competitors into a formerly monopolized market. To maintain control, BT announced it will not only sell its own phones (for the first time ever), but that BT's phones would come with plugs that fit into new sockets--also supplied, of course, by BT. If non-BT equipment is used, acquisition of these sockets will cost the consumer an additional £25.[15] In similar fashion, the Tripartite Accord cited above attempted to develop discriminatory standards for the fledgling European computer industries.

Design Standards: Case Studies

On a broader level, American exporters have encountered difficulties with standards based on design rather than performance. NTT's procurement of semiconductors, for example, is frequently based on design, with specifications often unfamiliar to foreign manufacturers. In some cases, designs are formulated by local Japanese producers through the development process and hence are considered proprietary.[16] Moreover, as noted above, changes or improvements in any product design necessitate resubmission for product approval. In West Germany, American computer manufacturers find health and safety standards often based on design. For example, one manufacturer claimed it was kept out of the German market for six months while it retooled to change the length of the keyboard. Such requirements certainly contravene the spirit of the Standards Code. The greatest damage, of course (and this is impossible to measure), stems from manufacturers' decisions to not export their products because of the retooling that design standards require. Entire markets may be lost as a result.

Transparency Issues: Case Studies

Design standards could be replaced by performance-related requirements on an international scale if transparent procedures for new and amended standards and certification systems became more prevalent. Under the Standards Code, signatories are obligated to inform one another of proposed additions or changes to existing standards at an early stage, as well as the rationales and objectives behind the new proposals. Moreover, fellow-signatories are to be given a reasonable amount of time to respond on the proposal before it goes into effect, with the purpose of suggesting amendments to minimize the standard's effect on trade. While in theory this process could eliminate barriers such as design standards, the reality is far different.

American firms generally have little access to the Japanese standard-writing process. Opportunity for formal comment often comes far too late in the process to be meaningful. As a result, Japanese standards often give little consideration to foreign products. Moreover, Japanese producers generally are aware of changes in standards and certification systems well before foreign manufacturers, and thus are able to effect the required product changes while foreign producers must wait for the official announcement. In the case of the EEC, proposed standards directives are conveyed to the GATT just prior to their appearance in the EEC Official Journal. At this point, a consensus normally has emerged, and there is little opportunity for comment. (The EEC is not obligated under the Code to publish proposed directives at an earlier date.) In France, official decrees on standards are announced and go into effect at the same time.

Suggestions and Difficulties

The potential advantages to international trade of an accepted liberal system of standards in the high-technology industries have been a thread running through this analysis. Such a system would be based on reciprocal acceptance of test data, use of performance rather than design standards, and transparent procedures to encourage the development of international standards accepted by all countries. Such a system, given the present pace of technological change, has become necessary if only to extract the high-tech industries from the present confusion that is curbing their growth. A brief look at government and manufacturer initiatives in two industries, telecommunications and computers, demonstrates these present difficulties.

Recent developments in telecommunications have substantially merged the traditionally separate fields of user equipment and public communication resources. Computers now routinely communicate among themselves, while communication equipment has become computer-driven. This has unfortunately led to jurisdictional disputes between the international telecommunications standards-setting bodies (ISO and CCITT), with the result that the pace of product innovation has exceeded that of international agreement on the relevant standards. As indicated above, separate groups in the United States and Europe have now proposed their own systems, while the market giants (IBM and Xerox) have announced theirs. It is due to this competitive squabbling that the above-mentioned intercept system promulgated by the British has such a low probability of success. The result is that, in the new and fast-growing industry of value-added and local area networks, for example, most equipment is incompatible with similar but competitively produced products. The lack of commonly accepted standards acts as an effective disincentive to the use of foreign-produced systems.

Frustration over lack of common standards, and the reduced demand levels that result, has encouraged European computer manufacturers to agree on a common set of technical requirements to open the European market, at least among themselves. As it now stands, IBM sets the de facto standards, and the international standards that exist generally have not been applied. The ability of IBM to develop design standards has protected its market share--an apparently impenetrable position that rests in part on IBM's practice of not disclosing interface information. As has been the case in Japan, competitors have found this lack of information damaging to their efforts to produce IBM-compatible competitive equipment. This, in fact, was one of the central arguments in the antitrust case brought by the EEC Commission against IBM.[17]

It is significant, however, that the European producers seek to use their agreement as a tool for eroding IBM's market share. Their agreed-upon standards are not identical to IBM's. European producers here seek to turn the individual characteristic of IBM's standards into a disadvantage. Indeed, these manufacturers are already pressing EEC authorities to adopt their standards for future public procurement purposes.[18] The need for common standards in the computer industry is certainly a real one; it is simply characteristic of standards that the driving force behind the new European consensus has been a fear of IBM's growing market dominance. While the use of standards to specifically curb market share is illegitimate, past experience has shown it to be potentially effective.

GOVERNMENT PROCUREMENT

Definition

Governments are among the world's largest purchasers of goods. As such, they play a potentially significant role in international trade. Yet most of this vast market has traditionally been closed to foreign companies by formal and informal policies that discriminate in favor of national producers. Significant comparative advantage has been lost on an international scale as governments turned to often less-efficient domestic suppliers. While the development or maintenance of a firm or industry may be vital in the eyes of a government, it is noteworthy that local sourcing can be a comparatively inefficient means of achieving it. Direct subsidization of the weak link in the development/production process, for example, high capital costs associated with infrastructure development, is far more cost-effective. Despite this inefficiency, procurement policies are often pursued in product areas viewed as vital for both national security and the growth of other industries (electronics, computers and software). Thus, although government procurement may raise relative costs, political goals lead to their use in the development of today's fast-growing industries.[19]

The Procurement Code

In recognition of this barrier to trade and development, the issue of government procurement was one of the aforementioned six nontariff issues addressed in the Tokyo Round. Under the Agreement on Government Procurement (entering into force on April 1, 1981), American exporters theoretically have access to new markets worth some $25 billion.[20] The central tenet of the Agreement is the extension of the national treatment obligation of the GATT to government purchases. In awarding contracts, signatory governments are obligated to give equal treatment to foreign and domestic bids, and must apply the country-of-origin rules normally used for customs clearance. The specific governmental agencies of all signatories to which the Agreement applies also are identified (all state and local governments are excused from compliance). An important feature of the Agreement is its insistence on transparency in the procurement process, with specific guidelines to which signatories must adhere. Finally, the Committee on Government Procurement was established to facilitate implementation and assist in bilateral disputes.

Case Studies: Japan

Much of the attention in this field has fallen on France--whose drive to create national champions has led to a heavy emphasis on local sourcing--and on Japan. In the latter case, this may be attributed to Tokyo's succeeding where the French have not, and more importantly, to the comparatively large size of the Japanese government market. Until quite recently, American suppliers were not allowed to bid on GOJ purchases, and the issue was considered by some to be the most damaging NTB in America's trade with Japan.

Public corporations play an important role within the GOJ market, with some 115 state agencies active in the procurement process (which include, among others, the Nippon Telegraph and Telephone Corporation (NTT)). In the past (and, indeed, in the present) many of these corporations followed strict buy-Japanese policies. Perhaps more significantly, these state firms have developed joint R&D programs with private industry designed to develop those products later procured by the government. The result has been a closed circle in which R&D and procurement processes are insulated from non-Japanese corporations. Foreign access to both markets and technology is thereby curbed.[21]

Although the Procurement Code's coverage of Japanese governmental entities is substantially broader than that for most other Code signatories (and substantial progress has been made in opening up the Japanese procurement process), serious issues remain. Indeed, because of the potentially enormous sales involved (contrasted with an existing enormous American bilateral trade deficit with Japan) and the sensitive issue of competitiveness (coupled with perceived unfair Japanese practices), the issue of Japanese procurement in the advanced sectors is one of the few high-tech trade issues to emerge into the realm of high politics.

There are two examples of current Japanese procurement policies that are broadly representative of both the concerns surrounding procurement and the difficulties inherent in reducing this NTB. The first, Japan's satellite development program, has eliminated NTT procurement of foreign satellite systems in favor of a national effort to locally develop the requisite technology. Tokyo is not accepting international bids on satellite contracts,[22] and has stipulated that a domestic company must be the prime contractor on any new contracts.[23]

It is significant that American trade officials see this less as a procurement issue (although NTT is both the purchaser and largest user of procured satellites) and more as one of industrial subsidization. This perspective largely stems from the similarities between Japanese policies in the satellite industry and those policies successfully pursued by the GOJ in other sectors. For most of the 1970s, Japanese firms teamed up with American producers to acquire satellite-related technologies that would have been too expensive and time-consuming to develop on their own. While the GOJ continued to purchase foreign satellites, foreign satellite manufacturers increasingly turned to Japanese suppliers for components. Finally, in the fall of 1983, the government closed the satellite procurement market entirely to foreign suppliers.

This move fueled American concern with the development of a competitive Japanese satellite industry through local sourcing. Although the Japanese industry is certainly not in a position to export competitive satellite systems (it is unlikely this capacity can be attained even by 1990), it will play an increasingly important subcontracting role. Tokyo's procurement policies are therefore seen in Washington as not only closing a potentially large market, but as part of a targeting effort that, with the denial of market access, is attempting to build a competitive industry that will erode America's share of its own and third markets.

The second example, that of access to the Japanese telecommunications procurement market, involves an industry that is already competitive. At the end of 1983, the three-year open procurement agreement with NTT expired. Under this agreement, Japan had agreed to open its domestic telecommunications market (among the world's largest) to foreign competition. As the expiration date approached, USTR officials were initially reluctant to press for renewal.[24] Rather than opening the lucrative $3 billion/year NTT market, these officials claimed the agreement facilitated led to a major increase in Japanese sales to U.S. telephone companies (to fifteen times the level of comparative American sales to Japan).[25] Meanwhile, NTT did not purchase any mainline switching or computer equipment from American suppliers. After delaying the implementation of the agreement for one-and-one-half years, NTT purchased only basic equipment with a low technology content (e.g., telephones and telephone poles) from American suppliers.

In the renewal negotiations, White House negotiators did succeed in theoretically securing the participation of American companies in Japanese R&D cooperative arrangements, but this remains to be implemented. American manufacturers, moreover, are generally pessimistic on their chances of gaining access into the closed circle of the R&D/procurement process, citing the privatization of NTT as a means of enabling the company to escape these obligations.

Thus, the opening up of the Japanese telecommunications procurement market has somewhat surprisingly met with mixed reaction from American suppliers. While many have been skeptical of NTT's sincerity, other American firms were split internally in their support, with overseas divisions favoring marketing efforts opposed at home. Obviously, American marketing executives still harbor a good deal of suspicion over NTT's willingness to procure from non-Japanese firms--a pessimistic view attributable to most American suppliers and one that has encouraged American firms to enter into partnerships with local Japanese companies. Indeed, there is evidence that NTT itself was split in its support for the agreement, and resistance at the middle-management level may have prompted the rejection of some American bids. Yet in fairness to NTT, some misguided American firms attempted to exploit Washington's pressure on Tokyo, and made heavy-handed and counterproductive allusions to the political considerations of NTT's procurement decisions.

Most interesting to this analysis are those American firms that made a competitive and concerted effort to penetrate the NTT market. In facing an entirely new market, these firms have needed time (estimated at about three years) to acquaint themselves with new procedures such as maintaining an in-country presence, translating documents, and possibly modifying products for sale to NTT. NTT's market is highly competitive, and the traditional family of Japanese suppliers in the field is accustomed to the particular Japanese standards and requirements. Consequently, once an American firm incurs the considerable expense of a marketing effort, it is by no means guaranteed success. One American supplier estimated its cost to maintain a one-person office in Japan at $400,000 annually, with no guarantee of a return. Not surprisingly, American telecommunications suppliers supported a renewal of the procurement agreement. Given the difficulties involved in start-up operations, there is a consensus among these firms that three years has been too short a period to show significant results.[26]

Case Studies: France

French procurement practices are broadly similar to the Japanese examples cited above. Recently, the French announced that, in the case of computer purchases, the government market will be opened. Interestingly, the impetus for this move was less international pressure than a belated recognition that IBM-France was in a better position than Honeywell-Bull to maintain employment--an overriding national concern. Admitting that a rigid buy-French attitude has in the past squandered resources, the GOF now insists that nationalized Bull concentrate on market niches.[27]

Yet the reality remains uncertain. When Mitterand entered office in 1981, he created an intragovernmental consulting group, the Research Center for Administrative Information Systems (CESIA), that has matched government orders in the information technology field with domestic suppliers. Moreover, strict rules-of-origin remain in place, and encourage local sourcing of foreign-made components used in the manufacturing process; hence, the present uncertain situation where public-sector users can theoretically choose their own equipment, while foreign manufacturers find penetration of the government market difficult.[28] Similar and persistent difficulties are found in the PTT's procurement of switching and transmission equipment. Two government-sanctioned supplier cartels supply this market. As strict technology-transfer requirements are a prerequisite to foreign entry into these cartels (local R&D facilities must be constructed and include French participation), non-French bidding for these contracts is reduced substantially.

As is the case with the Japanese satellite industry, the French government has resorted to the procurement process in order to develop selected market niches. Particularly in the fields of the computer and electronic measuring instruments industries, the GOF has placed contracts with selected firms even if they did not produce the relevant products. A selected firm uses the signed development contract to secure low-interest commercial loans that are then used for both R&D and production purposes. Procurement, again, plays a critical role in the government's targeting efforts.[29]

The implications here for American corporate strategy are far-reaching. In order to secure an advantage in the French marketplace, American firms operating in targeted sectors recognize that they must become the most 'French' in their industry. Once a national champion is selected and producing the product line, foreign competition will be hamstrung by GOF procurement policies and other NTBs. Yet, the cost of becoming French is high. It may involve an increase in local sourcing, resulting in higher costs and diminished export competitiveness. Or it may require a joint venture with the selected national champion. Profitability is difficult to maintain, however, if this French firm has surplus manufacturing capacity (as is often the case). In this event, the American partner may be restricted to just one product from an entire product line, leaving the rest to French competitors.

Conclusion

As the preceding discussion suggests, the resistance found to opening government procurement lies both in public bodies and private firms. Governments may view procurement as an engine for development or as a means of maintaining assured supplies and stable market conditions in vital sectors. The Japanese certainly used national security arguments in resisting American pressures in the telecommunications sector. Yet, as has been seen when the procurement process was opened, risk-averse private firms have been reluctant to jump into new and uncertain markets. A wait-and-see attitude is, in retrospect, not surprising given the high start-up costs involved. This is not the view that USTR officials initially took in opposing the renewal of the NTT procurement agreement. Contrasted with the position taken by those firms attempting to penetrate the Japanese market, the USTR's position indicates it believed the obstacles to market entry lay solely in NTT's policies. As suggested above, the difficulties in opening procurement are broader and less prone to remedy through policy responses.

BARRIERS TO TRADE IN SERVICES

Definition

Trade in services can be affected by many barriers that are investment related, for example, barriers that limit the establishment of overseas subsidiaries, and by other obstacles that have both trade and investment elements. By erecting barriers to trade in services, governments can affect the development of high-technology sectors in two ways. First, by restricting data and information flows, they can directly affect the ability of firms to coordinate their operations; to have critical data on markets, products and competitors; and to establish important international facilities. Second, they can indirectly limit the operations of high-technology firms by restricting access to data they require to perform critical support operations such as insurance, construction, computer services and communications.

For most service firms, barriers can be quite varied. They can range from restrictions on investment to barriers that are related to both trade and investment. The barriers to trade in services that are related to investment include local labor laws that govern the licensing of professionals, mostly in law and accounting, but also in medicine (in biotechnology, medical licensing may constitute a direct barrier in some cases); discriminatory taxes; restrictions on remittances and the repatriation of profits; ownership restrictions; discriminatory regulatory requirements for bank reserves; and inadequate protection of intellectual property, trademarks, copyrights and technology. For software and computer services, inadequate laws can provide a key barrier for foreign firms that seek sales in markets where copyright protection does not exist.[30]

Other barriers are both trade and investment related. These include government subsidies, preferential treatment for government-controlled facilities, discriminatory licensing regulations, restrictions on importing goods essential for the use of service firms, discriminatory government procurement practices and an absence of internationally accepted standards for services.[31]

Transborder Data Flows

One of the most controversial problems of concern to high-technology firms is the issue of transborder data flows. As part of their effort to protect data collected on citizens, to limit access to local markets, and/or to promote the development of local telecommunications firms, a number of nations have placed limitations on the flow of data, on the use of specific types of information on private citizens and legal entities, or on the use of telecommunications equipment that is not produced locally. Although similar to regulatory policies, data flows have gained a life of their own in policy disputes.

While these restrictions have been tied to services, their ultimate impact is often on the sale and use of telecommunications equipment and data communications software. In many cases, as in Brazil,[32] the restrictions imposed on transborder data flows are primarily to promote the growth of an indigenous information industry, with concern ranging from computers to telecommunications equipment, software and modems. Restrictions on data flows or the offering of data processing services also limit investment in host nations by foreign service firms that would be substantial purchasers of such equipment and software such as banks, insurance companies, data processing and data service companies, securities firms, regional offices of multinational manufacturing firms, and law and accounting firms.

In Europe and Japan, the restrictions on transborder data flows are substantial. In Japan, private leased lines are available to data processing and data service vendors on the condition that the circuit be connected to only a single computer system in a single location abroad. In the Federal Republic of Germany, laws have been enacted to control the interconnection of private lines leased by multinational service and manufacturing companies. In

1981, Germany began to permit unprocessed data to be transmitted outside the FRG only if it came from other internationally leased circuits or from the national public data network. Under these laws, unprocessed data originating in Germany must first be processed locally before it can be transmitted internationally.[33] In 1982, German law began to restrict all companies from bringing international leased lines into Germany unless they terminated hard-wired into a single terminal device, or terminated in a computer system. To accompany this law, "substantial data processing is performed--in Germany--on the information transmitted over the international circuit, before it is distributed in Germany."[34] There also are restrictions that limit the resale and shared use of private lines, as well as the interconnection between private lines and a public switched network.

All of these restrictions are quite limiting to multinational users, especially companies providing data processing and information-based services. The controversy between Control Data Corporation (CDC) and the Japanese international record carrier Kokusai Denshin Denida Co., Ltd., or KDD, over provisions of a contract for a private leased line to transmit data between Japan and the United States is a good example of how limits on data flows affect high-technology sales. In limiting CDC's ability to transfer data between data processing centers in the United States and Japan, KDD restricted the number of services that CDC could offer in Japan by limiting the number of computer bases in the United States on which CDC could draw. KDD also required CDC to transfer its transmissions to a new usage-sensitive service from a private leased line, greatly raising its costs at some point in the future. This threatened to terminate or curtail CDC's ability to operate in Japan.[35] While this dispute has been settled, the restrictions were viewed by CDC as part of Japan's policy to "promote and exploit their data processing and telecommunications activities worldwide." This protection of Japan's industry was seen as only one part of an overall plan.[36]

Other barriers also are used to limit data flows.[37] The telecommunications ministries of governments in Europe charge substantially higher transatlantic rates for both private lines and switched circuits than do U.S. international record carriers. Restrictions on the connection of terminal equipment require government approval that must often be obtained from the government-owned telecommunications monopoly. Discriminatory technical standards for data communications services, such as standards for protocols in data communications, can be used to discriminate against foreign users by limiting the compatibility of U.S. and foreign equipment and software. Governments also have asserted their right to assure that certain sensitive data and data processing functions remain within their borders. They argue that there is a security risk or increased vulnerability to risk if such data leave the country. In addition, laws in many European nations limit the transborder transmission of computer-stored personal data in order to protect the privacy of their citizens, often requiring licensing procedures with reviews by public bodies that can deny permission to transmit information. In some nations, these laws extend to data about legal persons, corporations and unions, as well as private individuals.[38] Further concerns over transborder data flows have arisen in recent years over the use of direct broadcast satellite systems' cultural impacts and requirements that foreign subsidiaries of major U.S. corporations purchase their computer equipment and software locally.[39]

As mentioned earlier, restrictions on some firms' use of transborder data flows (Motorola, NCR, Xerox) are likely to increase their costs of operating overseas. This will result from the need to duplicate data, testing and information facilities. As such, it may reduce spending on R&D for products for the European market and is likely to reduce their future foreign investment outlays for Europe. Whether these restrictions will shift R&D spending into sectors that are unaffected by European data flow laws is difficult to judge. This should be clarified by further discussions with corporations that must comply with such legislation.

Services and International Trade Agreements

While services have not been included in the GATT Codes, efforts have been made by U.S. service firms to have them included in multilateral trade negotiations. In the Ford administration, pressure from the service industry resulted in the creation of high-level government interagency task forces to study service industries at the international level with special reference to GATT. The Carter administration subsequently decided to introduce services into the Tokyo Round. Very few types of services were included, however, and, then, only if linked to sales of goods. The new Codes to liberalize government procurement include those services incidental to the supply of products. The Tokyo Round also sought to limit government subsidies that distort trade. A number of these are related to services such as transportation subsidies to shipping firms. Government subsidies to services, however, were not made an explicit part of the new international rules.

In the November 1982 GATT ministerial meetings, the United States proposed a broad initiative on services. Because of poor advance preparation, this proposal failed to gain substantial support. It was greatly reduced in scope by the end of the meeting to just an invitation to have nations study trade in services, with the GATT secretariat playing a clearinghouse role. The United States had hoped for a formal agenda on services including an umbrella code and specific sectoral policies, where needed. The United States now hopes to get agreement to begin discussions for a new round of negotiations on trade in services at the Spring 1985 ministerial meeting. In order to succeed, however, it will have to put trade in services in a proper context relative to other trade issues.[40]

Thus, it has been difficult for nations to agree on the proper formula for the establishment of rules to govern trade in services. The political debate over transborder data flows, however, may result in a wider evaluation of the importance of having international agreements on trade in services. These would have to include such areas as the treatment of information flows that can affect key high-technology industries.

PERFORMANCE REQUIREMENTS

Definition

Trade-related performance requirements have become significant tools for governments to promote trade and local economic development. Reductions in tariffs and nontariff barrier codes that govern subsidies, dumping and government procurement resulting from the Tokyo Round of Multilateral Trade Negotiations (MTN) have limited the choices available to governments to protect markets. As a consequence, trade-related performance requirements have become a major way to subject foreign firms with equity and management participation in domestic companies to a variety of official policies. These measures are intended to increase the contribution of foreign firms to the host nation's trade and industrialization goals. Since they were not considered in MTN discussions and are not addressed in MTN codes, these measures have become an important tool to effect trade patterns and investment flows. This has occurred in spite of the fact that neither the articles nor the intent of the General Agreement on Tariffs and Trade (GATT) supports the use of government regulations as a means to discriminate against imports and in favor of domestic production.

Overview

There are two types of trade-related performance requirements: export performance requirements and local content requirements. Export performance requirements impose commitments on investing firms in a host nation "to export a fixed percentage of production or to export a specified minimum quantity of the goods produced."[41] These requirements artificially increase exports above prevailing levels and operate like an export subsidy. Local content requirements demand that a specific percentage of the value of goods produced by a foreign investor must be obtained locally or manufactured locally. Such steps promote local sourcing and increase the level of local value-added. They are similar in their impact to tariffs and import quotas. In a number of instances, these measures are not employed alone but are combined with additional requirements that can also distort trade. Investing firms may be required to avoid foreign exchange costs and, as a consequence, must balance exports and imports. In some instances, they may be required to have trade surpluses to earn foreign exchange for the host country. Local laws also can limit the remission of profits abroad or force firms to transfer technology to the host nation. If firms that desire to invest do not conform to these measures, they may not be permitted to invest in a country or be subjected to a broad range of penalties. On the other hand, firms that conform to performance requirements often receive substantial incentives.

Performance requirements usually are associated with developing nations and with the automobile sector. Ten percent of the overseas affiliates of U.S. corporations have reported being subjected to such policies, largely in Latin America.[42] Three to four percent of affiliates in developing countries have reported that they must conform to export or import requirements. But performance requirements are often used in developed countries in an exclusionary manner, limiting marketing entry. Thus, they can be used to protect local markets for national firms by limiting the entry of new competitors.

The ability of performance requirements to provide market protection appears to be quite important when we consider high-technology industries. In the Netherlands, local content requirements are occasionally applied to public and semipublic projects in high-technology areas.[43] U.S. firms selling electronics equipment in France have had to agree to use local components in order to win approval for investments. In Japan, electronics manufacturers have faced performance requirements intended to restrict competition in domestic markets. In the case of one U.S. firm, only after threats were made to cut off supplies of intermediate components to Japanese firms around the world and to refuse to license patents to Japanese competitors, was entry into Japan negotiated. U.S. firms also have encountered problems because of restrictions on the use of foreign components imposed by suppliers to Nippon Telephone and Telegraph in Japan.[44]

In the case of the developed nations, performance requirements may be an important tool used by governments to preserve the oligopolistic structure of domestic markets. While this may stifle innovation and reduce incentives to innovate, it does offer a shield to large domestic firms in high-technology industries that account for a large amount of employment.

One of the lessons learned from studies of local content legislation for the auto sector was that requirements vary depending on a government's development objectives. In autos, licensing and joint-venture agreements are usually used by nations that want to establish an industry through vehicle assembly operations. In this phase, two-tiered tariff structures and minimal local content requirements (35 percent or less) are used to support the development goals, with the lower tariffs levied on imported components used to assemble cars. Once domestic operations are established, government policies are usually focused on developing local parts producers, so domestic content requirements are increased. Often governments have sought to reduce the number of local producers in this phase in order to improve efficiency, to increase the scale of production and to gain a greater commitment from the remaining firms. In somes cases, these policies lead to disinvestment by foreign firms.[45]

In the third stage, after local industry can produce a wide range of components in addition to assembling vehicles, the policy direction often shifts again. Policies are more likely to encourage exports rather than import substitutions since governments are trying to achieve the higher economies of scale needed to compete in international markets. Export performance requirements are usually established in this phase and can be tied to more flexible domestic content regulations. Export requirements also may be linked to incentives for raising production volume, an approach used by Mexico and Brazil to increase auto exports in the 1970s.

Impacts

Performance requirements have the potential to change investment, export and R&D decisions by high-technology firms. By forcing U.S. firms to assemble goods locally, host nations impose additional costs that can result in inefficiencies. Because more funds must be devoted to host nation investment and to assisting in the development of local sources of components, U.S. companies may be forced to spend greater sums on direct investments and joint ventures and less on R&D.

In addition, local content requirements can give suppliers in host nations substantial market power and permit them to raise prices freely because of the noncompetitive structure of local markets. This can reduce the profitability of U.S. firms that have to operate in such markets and lessen their ability to finance new R&D. In such cases, U.S. firms may be required to do more of their R&D abroad. In some instances, U.S. supplier firms may find that their business in some foreign nations is lost because U.S. manufacturers must sign accords with local suppliers, as was mentioned above.

On the other hand, local content requirements may enable U.S. firms that are final producers to have their traditional domestic suppliers move into overseas markets. This would most likely be done through joint ventures, but might also involve management contracting, licensing agreements or direct investment. Such a move by traditional suppliers would enable them to enhance their profits on established products and would facilitate the development of global supply networks for U.S. multinationals.

LICENSING

Definition

Trade in the high-technology industries is significantly affected by licensing arrangements--more so, perhaps, than is trade of less technologically intensive goods--and is an issue of concern to governments and survival to exporters. There are two principal forms through which licensing with foreign entities normally takes place. First, there is the licensing of technologies and of production processes. This often takes the form of coproduction under performance requirements, or it may simply be a condition of market access. Second, there are the import licenses that governments often require in high-technology trade, and which may serve a multitude of purposes. These also may be one aspect of performance requirements that is used simply to restrict the inflow of intermediate goods. The relative dearth of information on this issue does, in fact, suggest that import licensing is used in conjunction with investment requirements. In this case, the affected American companies are very reluctant to approach Washington with their difficulties for fear of retaliation from the host government.

Overview and Case Studies

As with performance requirements, licensing arrangements are normally used to effect the transfer of technology and encourage the development of local industry. Better than quotas or tariffs, licenses monitor and regulate the flow of goods and technologies and are an effective tool for governments seeking to develop sectors within their economies. For example, foreign produced goods competing with those from a domestically targeted industry may be imported without restriction if the local manufacturers are not yet sufficiently capable of the necessary production levels on their own. Governments monitor these imports through automatic licensing arrangements. This provides policymakers with information concerning the foreign manufacturer, the type of product imported, and the level of those imports. It also provides the government with a relatively easy method of restricting those imports once a sufficient local capacity for production has been developed.

Technology licensing arrangements have received considerable attention this year due to Tokyo's proposals to impose licensing arrangements on imported (i.e., American) software. Not surprisingly, Washington found this completely unacceptable. The Japanese software industry is far behind its American counterpart, and MITI's proposals were widely seen as an attempt to build a competitive Japanese industry upon patented American technologies. MITI's new policies would, first, place a fifteen-year limit on any importer's right to protect his software with a patent (it is now protected for fifty years), and, second, require a company to license any program used in Japan (and thereby disclose confidential information) where disclosure would be in the public interest of the Japanese.[46]

Access to the Japanese software market thus could require a substantial transfer of software technology. Washington resisted these measures in repeated and often heated exchanges with MITI representatives. Critics also noted that, if passed, these policies would likely curb the availability of needed American software. This would likely reduce Japanese demand for computers and related components, and thus could have a braking effect on Japan's entire electronic equipment industry. Prospects for the proposed legislation are now unclear.

Considerable attention also has been generated by the proposed use of operating licenses to regulate Japan's newly opened secondary services market (chiefly value-added networks (VAN)). This proposal surfaced in a major turf battle between MITI and the Ministry of Post and Telecommunications (MPT).[47] MITI would have preferred to have jurisdiction over this market and deny MPT any role whatsoever, while MPT sought to create a role for itself by regulating value-added networks through licensing arrangements. While technically these were to be operating licenses, they would have regulated an ongoing service industry, and restricting them would have had an effect identical to that of tightening an import licensing arrangement for manufactured goods. Indeed, MPT based its proposal in part on the need to develop this infant Japanese industry. Again, the status of these proposals is uncertain.

The two examples cited above, where licensing arrangements were proposed but not enacted, are significant in that they demonstrate Tokyo's use of licensing arrangements to either encourage the development of an industry (software) or to potentially protect a relatively competitive market from destabilizing foreign competition (value-added networks). These objectives are precisely those found earlier in the case of GOJ procurement. At the very least, this pattern would suggest that Tokyo has attempted to achieve trade-related goals through licensing arrangements.

Indeed, today's Japanese high-tech firms owe much of their startling development to their American competitors who, in the 1970s, provided the Japanese with advanced technologies in exchange for a degree of market access. For example, in the case of the semiconductor industry, Tokyo's restrictions on foreign investment led American manufacturers in the 1970s to enter into licensing agreements with Japanese producers. The Japanese market was potentially enormous (and is now second only to that of the United States), and American firms saw licensing arrangements as the only feasible method of gaining access. Nor was this irrational, for these American firms were reasonably sure--in the short run--that their technology would not be used in products competing in their own markets. An interesting exception was Texas Instruments (TI), which held a series of fundamental patents on ICs. Being in a stronger position than most American firms, TI became the only American semiconductor firm to successfully negotiate approval for a wholly owned Japanese subsidiary (a multipart agreement that was finally realized in 1972). In exchange, TI agreed to license its patents to Japanese firms. Similarly, just as TI became the only American firm to manufacture and market semiconductors in Japan, IBM had--on the strength of its patents--become the only American company in this period to build computers there.

These types of restrictive licensing arrangements persist, although now this situation has been largely reversed. After the clear success of MITI's VLSI project (initiated in 1976), which resulted in over 1,000 patents, the Japanese semiconductor industry was in some respects even more competitive than its American counterpart. In order to compete in the Japanese VLSI market, U.S. firms would have required access to the technology developed through the MITI project. Yet only two American firms have been granted licenses for these patents--and these agreements were tied to cross-licenses in other areas. As a result, the five major Japanese semiconductor companies participating in the VLSI project have received free access to technologies that, through their lack of accessibility to foreign companies, have created markets insulated from American competition.[48]

Conversely, a rarer example of technology licensing is the marketing of a technology without significant access to the market it supplies. For example, in 1975 the French government recognized the failure of its Le Plan Calcul, and decided to pressure Honeywell to merge its French operations with the nationalized CII-Bull computer firm. In 1982, CII-Honeywell was nationalized by the Mitterand government. In exchange for licenses to its patented technologies, Honeywell reportedly received a considerable sum. Yet, Honeywell was also largely excluded from the French market--a market that continued to rely on Honeywell's technologies.

The Licensing Code

GATT attention in the Tokyo Round focused only on import licenses. Although this is only one of many licensing-related NTBs in the high-tech industries, it is the most amenable to international treatment. The GATT Licensing Code (effective January 1, 1980) does not deal with specific arrangements, but addresses the administration of import licensing systems and attempts to minimize trade impacts by simplifying and harmonizing import regulation. For example, it stipulates that importers should normally have to approach only one administrative body, and that a reasonable period should be allowed for applications. Automatic licensing (where import licenses are granted freely) systems should be maintained only as long as the circumstances that gave rise to them exist, or if the administrative objective cannot be met by a more reasonable method.[49]

Unfortunately, the Licensing Code is weakly worded, and few countries have notified the GATT of alleged violations.[50] As has been seen, licensing difficulties that involve high-technology trade range far beyond import licensing issues. Stipulating stringent and technology transferring conditions for market access, moreover, does not violate the Code.

Monitoring

One of the greatest difficulties in examining licensing as a possible NTB is the scarcity of relevant information. As was suggested in the opening paragraph, this is because restrictive licensing arrangements are likely an integral aspect of performance requirements. Companies that enter into local-sourcing agreements with host governments do so because it is often the only avenue toward market access. These firms are unwilling to jeopardize that arrangement by complaining to Washington of the specific performance requirements operating in the country. The local government, meanwhile, enforces its local-sourcing arrangements through import licensing procedures that can be tightened once the transfer of technology and/or coproduction of the intermediate good is realized. More efficient foreign suppliers of intermediate goods are left wondering what happened to earlier demand levels as their corporate customers shift supplies. Normally these intermediate manufacturers are not even aware of the array of licensing arrangements, ranging from simple import licenses to more complex technology-transfer agreements, that have been entered into and that have transferred demand to local markets. Nor, for that matter, are U.S. trade officials informed.[51]

NOTES

1. Robert E. Baldwin, Non-Tariff Distortions of International Trade (Brookings Institution, 1970).
2. USTR, "International Trade Issues in Telecommunications, Data Processing, and Information Services" (unpublished).
3. From interviews with officials at USTR, April/May 1984.
4. Interview with Donald Abelson, Director, Technical Trade Barriers, USTR, May 17, 1984; U.S. Dept. of Commerce, International Trade Administration, The Telecommunications Industry (April 1983).
5. Other codes were for subsidies and countervailing measures, antidumping, government procurement, customs valuation and import licensing. It is noteworthy that a country, while signing the main body of the Tokyo Round, may at its discretion opt out of signing the individual codes.
6. U.S. Department of Commerce, International Trade Administration, Technical Barriers to Trade, Vol. 4 (September 1981).

7. Notable omissions are that the Code's provisions are not applicable to standards involving services, those included in government procurement contracts, or those established by companies for their own use.

8. USTR officials claim that until very recently the Japanese did not accept foreign test data for any product that was imported. This may now be changing, although prospects remain uncertain. "Foreign Test Data To Be Accepted," Journal of Japanese Trade and Industry (May/June 1984); "Miami Lab to Certify U.S. Goods for Sale in Japan," New York Times (May 23, 1984).

9. Japanese Non-Tariff Barriers: A Selective Evaluation (A. T. Kearney, International, Inc., May 30, 1982).

10. Office of the U.S. Special Trade Representative, Report to the U.S. Congress on the Agreement on Technical Barriers to Trade--Standards Code, January 1980/December 1982 (1982).

11. Japanese Non-Tariff Barriers.

12. JIS Guide 84, Part I, Japanese Standards Association, Ministry of International Trade and Industry, p. 5.

13. "Bizarre Standards Confusion," Financial Times (March 5, 1984).

14. "When the Planning Has To Stop," New Scientist (December 2, 1982).

15. "British Telecom Connects with the Retail Industry," New Scientist (November 26, 1981).

16. The Effect of Government Targeting on World Semiconductor Competition, Semiconductor Industry Assoc. (January 1983).

17. Hans Braggaar, "European Antitrust Case Against IBM Still on Books," Computer World (April 30, 1984).

18. "Europe's Computer Groups Forge Pact," Financial Times (March 16, 1984).

19. Abel Farnoux, Excerpts from the Report by the Committee for Electronics (Paris: French Ministries of State and of Research and Technology, March 1982).

20. U.S. Department of Commerce, International Trade Administration, Government Procurement, Vol. 2 (July 1981).

21. USTR, Japanese Barriers to U.S. Trade and Recent Japanese Government Trade Initiatives (November 1982); Electronic Industries Association, "Changes in U.S. Telecommunications Industry and Impact on U.S. Telecommunications Trade," Submission to the International Trade Commission, April 17, 1984.

22. This policy does not technically violate the Procurement Code. The procuring governmental entity, the National Space Development Agency, is not specifically identified in the Code's appendixes and is thus exempt from the provisions.

23. "Japan's Satellite Development Program," JEI Report (March 16, 1984).

24. Interview with David Shark, Director of Government Procurement, Office of GATT Affairs, USTR, May 17, 1984; Inside U.S. Trade (September 5, 1983).

25. It is questionable whether the agreement played a significant role in increased Japanese telecommunications exports--at the time of the signing, the United States already had a substantially open market.

26. General Accounting Office, Assessments of Bilateral Telecommunications Agreements with Japan (October 7, 1983).

27. Nevertheless, in 1982 French manufacturers had a 63 percent share of the civil service's installed base (versus a private market share of 45 percent). U.S. Department of Commerce, International Trade Administration, The Computer Industry (April 1983).

28. "France Blends Technology, Socialism," High Technology (November 1983); "IBM and Mitterand--An Entente Cordial," Financial Times (November 28, 1983).

29. "Non-Tariff Barrier Analysis," computerized data base maintained through 1977 by USTR.

30. Ronald K. Shelp, Beyond Industrialization: Ascendancy of the Global Service Economy (New York: Praeger Publishers, 1981), p. 111.

31. Ibid., p. 112.

32. United Nations, Centre on Transnational Corporations, Transborder Data Flows and Brazil (New York: United Nations, 1983).

33. Office of the U.S. Trade Representative, "Selected Problems Encountered by U.S. Service Industries to Trade in Services," computerized listing, May 11, 1983, p. 49.

34. U.S., Congress, House, Committee on Government Operations, Subcommittee on Government Information and Individual Rights, International Data Flow (Washington, D.C.: U.S. Government Printing Office, 1980), p. 21.

35. Ibid., pp. 21-22.

36. Testimony of Hugh P. Donahue of Control Data Corporation in U.S. Congress, House, Committee on Government Operations, International Data Flow, p. 25.

37. U.S., Congress, Senate, Committee on Commerce, Science and Transportation, Long-Range Goals in International Telecommunications and Information: An Outline for United States Policy (Washington, D.C.: U.S. Government Printing Office, 1983), pp. 170-171.

38. U.S., Congress, House, Committee on Interstate and Foreign Commerce, Subcommittee on Communications, Inter-

national Barriers to Data Flows: Background Report (Washington, D.C.: U.S. Government Printing Office, 1979).

39. U.S., Congress, Senate, Committee on Government Operations, International Information Flow: Forging a New Framework (Washington, D.C.: U.S. Government Printing Office, 1980), pp. 14-27, 31-36; Jane Bortnick, International Telecommunications and Information Policy: Selected Issues for the 1980s (Washington, D.C.: U.S. Government Printing Office, 1983), pp. 21-25.

40. Jeffrey Schott, "The GATT Ministerial: A Postmortem," Challenge (May/June 1983), pp. 40-45.

41. The Labor-Industry Coalition for International Trade (LICIT), Performance Requirements (Washington, D.C.: LICIT, March 1981), p. 2.

42. Ibid.

43. Ibid., p. 4.

44. A. T. Kearney, International, Inc., Japanese Non-Tariff Barriers: A Selective Evaluation (Tokyo: Kearney Management Consultants, May 30, 1980), p. 90.

45. U.S. Department of Commerce, International Trade Administration, Office of International Sector Policy, "An Analysis of Automobile Local Content Laws in Other Countries" (October 1983), pp. 1-2.

46. Inside U.S. Trade (March 9, 1984).

47. Japan Economic Institute, JEI Report (March 16, 1984).

48. International Trade Commission, Foreign Industrial Targeting and Its Effects on U.S. Industries, Phase I: Japan (October 1983).

49. USTR, A Preface to Trade (1982).

50. Interview with Florizelle Liser, USTR, May 17, 1984.

51. Interview with Beverly Vaughan, International Economist, USTR, May 17, 1984.

4
The Impact of NTBs on Corporate Decisionmaking

OVERVIEW

Nontariff barriers pose problems for firms that dwarf those associated with tariffs. The barriers, even when designed to deliberately restrict trade, are often subtle, invisible, imposed intermittently and not subject to quantification. The mere process of fact-finding is thereby tremendously complicated. Particularly with respect to high-technology industries, NTBs are a moving target. They evolve with rapid changes in technology and in market structure that characterize leading-edge industries. Government trade officials are unlikely to possess either the technical expertise or the resources to monitor such changeable restrictions. This is reflected in the poor quality of U.S. government data bases on NTBs, which tend to routinely be at least two years out of date.

Corporate decisionmakers seeking to gain access to a potentially lucrative market are often faced with an array of barriers to market entry. Given the problems of invisibility, subtlety and such noted above, they are unlikely to have anticipated the nature and extent of these barriers before committing the firm to the market; nor is the legality of these measures likely to be clear, given the ambiguity in NTB trade law as well as of the NTB itself. Indeed, questions of legality may not even occur to the corporate official who tends to view such restrictions as part of the ordinary cost of doing business. His problem may be compounded by the dispersion of authority and plethora of government agencies he has to deal with in the foreign country (or in Washington, should he choose to lodge a complaint). He may find himself emeshed in long and inconclusive negotiations as differences among foreign government agencies are reconciled, and as the NTB itself changes in response to pressures from domestic firms. Thus, should the corporation choose to negotiate the removal or amelioration of the barrier, it can usually count on an extended period of uncertainty and a raising of the ante as negotiations proceed, with no assurance that unacceptable demands will not be made at the very end of negotiations.

Our research indicates that NTBs have greater impacts on smaller firms than on larger ones because of the less-extensive international presence of most small businesses, their lack of sophistication in international trade matters, and the lack of resources such companies can devote to responding to NTBs. This problem is critical because small firms in a rapid growth stage need an unlimited access to markets to regain the funds they have invested in new products and services as quickly as possible. It also is important since NTBs can prevent small firms with high-quality products and services from establishing themselves in markets that can make important contributions to their growth. Not being a first entrant in foreign markets can result in loss of a significant amount of current and future business.

Larger firms are often more successful in responding to NTBs because they have staffs and operations in many foreign markets. As a consequence, they often have foreign nationals working for their firm who know which parts of foreign governments must be visited to negotiate a way around an NTB. These foreign staffs have often invested much time in establishing such contacts and gaining a careful familiarity with the practices and customs of a host nation. A small firm hoping to enter these markets does not have this staff to draw upon and often cannot commit a great amount of resources to obtaining approval for its product or service when an NTB is involved. As a result, the costs of reacting to an NTB may make it unprofitable for a smaller firm to enter a foreign market. It may withdraw and lose sales that could have contributed to its growth because the costs of dealing with an NTB are too high.

One way to continue to try to serve such a market in spite of NTBs would be to license the product or enter a joint venture with a local partner. This can be a way of obtaining some profits from foreign sales to blocked markets. However, such loss of control to foreign partners may be detrimental to small firms since they can lose knowledge of the new demands emerging in the marketplace that may be addressed by the foreign licensee, rather than the U.S. firm. Over the medium term, this can lead to a loss of business and diminish the competitiveness of the U.S. firm. Since setting up a facility in a foreign country to help overcome an NTB is often too costly for smaller firms, direct foreign investment may not be a suitable alternative to licensing and joint ventures.

Marketing arrangements can also be limited by NTBs. If NTBs make it difficult to deliver a final product or establish a service network, a small U.S. firm may be forced to work through a larger U.S. company to market its product or service. Again, this results in a loss of control and less familiarity with a foreign market. It also retards the development of important international marketing skills in the small firm. If such skills are not developed, U.S. exports can decline and smaller U.S. firms may be less likely to venture into foreign markets. In addition, they may fail to develop skills in finding export financing, export trading companies, and other support services required to be successful abroad.

Because of a lack of resources, smaller firms are at a disadvantage in redesigning or adapting products and services to foreign markets. However, this problem may turn out to be an advantage for small firms, in spite of the costs, if they are more flexible than larger companies in redesigning products and making decisions rapidly.

QUESTIONS CONCERNING THE IMPACT OF NTBs ON CORPORATE DECISIONMAKING

We assembled a lengthy list of questions to guide our evaluation of the impacts of NTBs on the decisions of U.S. corporations. These are presented here in outline form, followed by a discussion of the results of our interviews, case studies and panel discussions.

I. R&D Impacts

A. R&D Location

1. Is R&D located in host nations in order to gain information about future regulations, standards, and acceptance criteria so that development of new products occurs with these limitations in mind?
2. Can R&D be located in host nations in response to barriers to market entry?

    a. This may be due to a government's attempts to get a transfer of technology or of skills to the local population (Brazil's computer and data processing industries).
    b. It may also occur because local manufacturing is blocked unless there is an R&D branch established locally.

B. R&D Design

1. Are R&D designs modified to conform to new standards, local current requirements and other criteria?

   a. This can lead to R&D personnel being shifted back to the United States because of their familiarity with foreign standards.
   b. It can lead to greater dependence on automated design and manufacture (CAD/CAM) because of size, time, and complexity limitations.
   c. It can also lead to a radical departure in product conceptualization; global, modularized products may be the result.

2. Has centralizing R&D design in the U.S. led to a need to reassess the benefit of carrying out R&D in host nations, particularly major markets?

   a. This may lead to a confrontation with some foreign governments that view R&D in high technology as a determinant of national security (France, Japan).
   b. It also may lead corporations to consolidate their R&D networks, perhaps pulling them back into regional centers rather than having a system of national centers.

C. R&D Spending/Allocation

1. Must products be modified to conform to new criteria or costly standards? The first stage of modularization is likely to be costly.
2. Does moving R&D back to the U.S. increase R&D costs due to higher personnel and facilities costs?
3. Are there cases where a company walks away from an already-developed product, before it can be marketed, due to NTBs?
4. Do companies revise R&D spending programs to shift funds away from products that will perform less well because certain markets are blocked by NTBs?

   a. This reallocation of R&D funds is likely to be at the direction of a high-level corporate manager, rather than by a director of corporate R&D.

II. Marketing Impacts

While marketing barriers are often not directly tied to government-supported regulations (a key exception being the French and Japanese VCR dispute), inaction on the part of governments to liberalize marketing arrangements can act as an important NTB. Overcoming such a barrier may not only be costly, but may result in a delay in the time it takes for a high-tech firm to enter a foreign market. This time delay is very critical because attaining a good share of a foreign market often depends upon whether a firm is one of the first entrants.

A. Marketing Strategy

1. How is marketing strategy handled and how are products designed so that modifications can be made easily in order to respond to changes in market conditions?

   a. While the size of demand is often uncertain for high-tech products, barriers to foreign markets can increase the scale of uncertainty and likelihood that expectations will not be accurately predicted by marketing research. How do firms respond?
   b. If distribution systems are difficult to establish, firms may need to give up some control in order to gain timely entry into a market through licensing, offset arrangments, etc. Does this occur very often?
   c. Are new forms of investment a consequence of the problems faced by firms in marketing high-tech products in foreign markets--joint ventures, close links to trading companies, more extensive licensing?

III. Impacts on Investment

A. Investment Location

1. Is the location of investment determined by market access requirements? In order to secure a viable market share, a company may be required to invest a specified amount in the host country.

   a. Are there companies that, in order to become national champions (the only viable method of maintaining market share), decide they must source a greater amount of inputs locally? This involves, however, higher costs and decreased competitiveness for exports.

b. Investing in facilities in the local market provides companies with a presence not obtainable through marketing activities. This enables the company to:

- Increase its influence over the development of local design standard specs for a product.
- Learn of impending changes in govenment policy affecting its market sooner than foreign firms with no manufacturing presence.
- Improve the chance of marketing to the government, or of convincing other consumers that the company offers a more stable supply than do other foreign firms with no manufacturing presence (e.g., the case of sophisticated electronics, which are often subject to U.S. export restraints).

2. Are problems created when countries require foreign investors to place a plant in an economically depressed region?

   a. Most European countries presently provide public assistance to encourage firms to locate in these regions--and occasional stories have surfaced where government agencies have conducted some arm-twisting to ensure it.

B. Investment Characteristics

1. How does the requirement by the host government that technology be licensed in return for allowing a company to set up manufacturing facilities in that country affect investment decisions by U.S. firms?
2. Are joint ventures an important condition for market access, at least for successful market access, as is the case in France with the national champions?
3. Are employment requirements that are placed on new investments and local sourcing requirements an important cause of higher costs and decreased export competitiveness for these local facilities?

   a. Decreased control over the production process may distort that process, creating bottlenecks in supplies and added costs to ensure that adequate local suppliers can be found or developed.

- Foreign production facilities thus become vulnerable to events that would not necessarily affect production in the company's own domestic facilities.

4. Are export requirements placed on new facilities? This if often the case with countries experiencing balance-of-payment difficulties, for example, France. How does this affect investment decisions?

   a. This may lead to difficulties in third markets because the company must increase its market share in these third markets if it is to fully utilize its productive facilities.

IV. Impacts on Exporting

A. Customs

1. Do customs difficulties appear to be arbitrary (i.e. differ from port-of-entry to port-of-entry) or be based on policy?

   a. Do arbitrary difficulties, such as in the case of identical products that pass at one entry point but not at another, create uncertainties for exporters that diminish their products' attractiveness to local distributors who can obtain greater reliability from local suppliers?
   b. Do policy-based difficulties, such as the Japanese tolerance for extensive testing of backlogs at customs (up to two years in some cases), create higher costs and uncertainties as to the delivery date to market that affect corporate decisions?

      - In some instances, these delays have been so significant and critical that Japanese manufacturers have been able to use the delay to get their own competitive products to market and thereby eliminate the potential market advantage of the American company.

B. Certification

1. Do lengthy and/or costly certification procedures result in decreased export competitiveness for an American

company, or do they keep that company out of the foreign market altogether?

a. The German Society of Engineers has developed rigorous standards for the computer industry, but does not allow self-certification. German engineers must instead be brought to the United States, at the American company's expense, to witness the testing procedures.

2. Do certification requirements serve to strengthen a cultural advantage of local producers?

a. American exporters cannot apply directly to the government for product approval, but must instead use a Japanese agent. This serves to strengthen the already substantial control that Japanese distributors hold over the distribution of American exports in Japan.

A REVIEW OF THE IMPACTS OF NTBs ON CORPORATE DECISIONMAKING

I. R&D Impacts

A. R&D Location

A number of U.S. companies, especially large firms, verified that they had located R&D operations in host nations to gain information about future regulations, standards or acceptance criteria. This often is a defensive reaction, protecting the U.S. firm from losing out on access to information about crucial changes in regulations, some of which may have required costly changes in product design if they were not known early in a product's development. In nations such as France and Italy, the need to have local R&D operations is particularly important.

R&D operations can also be located in host nations in response to NTBs or market barriers. One case was mentioned by a panelist in our study, who cited the use of duty uplift fees on parts as a device to increase local production and/or local R&D. Such fees impose higher charges on parts needed by a U.S. company's local subsidiary.

B. R&D Design

One case illustrative of changes in R&D design was an electronics company that altered the design of its earth station equipment so that it could be modularized to conform to various local frequency requirements through the addition of modules. In order to produce such a modularized product, the U.S. company shifted R&D personnel from overseas operations back to the United States and relied much more on CAD/CAM to save time in designing the complex new product.

This sort of response also is described in the case on standards and procurement affecting marketing, sales and R&D. A major American manufacturer of computer and communications equipment was surprised when the European PTTs did not opt for the gradual adoption of a new packet-switching protocol, X.25, but made it the protocol for the entire communications system. As a result, foreign competitors who had not yet developed equipment compatible with the X.25, like this American company, were kept out of the market. The PTTs may have had several reasons for stipulating that the X.25 support entire systems. Most European manufacturers were ahead of their American counterparts in developing the requisite equipment; once the X.25 became the standard for the industry, the only qualifying suppliers were predominantly European. Moreover, the market giant, IBM, utilized a different architecture, SNA. By requiring all equipment to support the X.25, the PTTs may have hoped to give their own industries a significant share of this market before IBM could bring its own product lines into conformance with X.25.

Development of the equipment compatible with this protocol became a top priority in the American company's R&D facilities in the United States (where all of its R&D is conducted). Because of the technical complexity of the design, this company thought a licensing arrangement with a European concern that had already developed the equipment was inappropriate.

Company personnel operating in the European market were brought home to expedite the development process and ensure compatibility with the European standards. As technical requirements for the protocol differed somewhat among the major European markets, the American company chose to modularize the design so that slight modifications could be made to suit each market.

The company also faced difficult NTBs over type-certification (where once the model or design is certified, testing is not required on each individual and identical piece of equipment) for sale in Europe.

C. R&D Spending/Allocation

There are several cases, primarily in the telecommunications industry, where products or services had to be modified to conform to new standards or where R&D spending had been discouraged because of NTBs. In one clear instance, a U.S. Fortune 500 firm had refused to spend additional funds on R&D because markets were blocked by NTBs.

In this case, a subsidiary of a major Fortune 500 firm sold a telecommunications product to a small number of foreign governments. Because these governments are very interested in having telecommunications technology transferred to their own national companies, they often purchase just the components rather than the final product, and their buy-national policies have for all practical purposes closed off their markets to final product sales. As a consequence, the U.S. firm, which in the absence of discrimination would conduct R&D targeted at foreign sales, will allocate little or no R&D funds to becoming a leader in the telecommunications technology required abroad, concentrating instead on sales to the U.S. market and innovative projects that can be funded by the Department of Defense. It may be unrealistic to expect that the firm would devote substantial funds to foreign markets now, since U.S. markets are growing so rapidly. It is, however, likely that this firm would focus on foreign markets once U.S. growth stabilizes if there were no discrimination. The firm also has developed unique marketing practices to obtain component sales abroad, working through trading companies in Japan and industrial partners in Europe.

The NTBs faced by this firm are largely the result of national policies to promote the growth of selected high-technology sectors. While the telecommunications product it sells is difficult to market abroad, because of closed government procurement markets, the U.S. firm plays an important role as an original equipment manufacturer (OEM), or component supplier, for foreign companies. Because of its expertise, it participates in joint ventures with foreign companies since it knows how to lower the costs of producing the final product and is expert in managing production, thus lowering the risks of producing faulty products.

This situation is somewhat relaxed when the final product is procured by a quasi-government agency or an entity that is more independent of existing government controls. In such cases, the U.S. firm's final product is more likely to win in competitions with products of foreign companies because of clear advantages in price and performance. However, there has been at least one case where a much smaller foreign component firm has won a competition with the U.S. company because of its familiarity with the standards requirements of a Western European government.

Nevertheless, a company executive believes that since the number of buyers for the final product is extremely small, governments do not have to establish a broad range of NTBs. Rather, they can utilize a buy-national approach that leads agencies and national companies to buy only components and not the final product. The governments appear to assume that the benefits of this policy far outweigh the liabilities, because employment is being generated in high-technology sectors and important skills are being developed in national firms. There are some differences among governments where purchases of U.S. goods are more likely because of deregulation of state PTTs. The more independent the new authorities are from the state, the more likely they are to purchase U.S.-produced products.

As a consequence of these policies, the U.S. firm does not do any R&D for overseas markets and exports only products developed in the United States. While the U.S. company could do research that would put it in a key position in foreign markets because of the complexity of its product and the details of producing it, it has not. Rather, it focuses on innovative products required by U.S. customers. Recently, it developed an innovative power supply that has been marketed to an international agency and then sold abroad. However, when the U.S. firm plans its own R&D program, it does not target anything for the Japanese, European, and developing nations' markets, where it has little potential for business. Instead, it tries to trigger U.S. government funding for innovative products, often from the Defense Department.

II. Marketing Impacts

A. Marketing Strategy

A number of cases we discussed with corporate executives concerned the impact of NTBs on marketing practices and strategics. In a number of cases, NTBs, such as the refusal to award a patent on a new telecommunications product of a U.S. firm, blocked access to foreign markets.

In this case, a U.S. company developed a new telecommunications product that it patented in the United States in 1970 and in Europe from 1971 to 1973. It was unable to receive a patent on the product in Japan because, in the company's opinion, the Japanese wanted to develop their own product as an integral part of Japan's strategy in telecommunications.

The U.S. firm commercialized the product through joint ventures with Siemens and others in the EEC and tried to sell it in Japan in the early 1970s to NTT, the Japanese phone company.

NTT refused. In order to get into the Japanese market, the company tried to form a joint venture with Japanese partners, but the Japanese companies said that NTT would not approve of such an arrangement. Consequently, the product was developed in Japan, by a Japanese firm.

The U.S. firm believes that the Japanese infringed on its patent rights and used Japan's refusal of a patent to keep it out of the Japanese market. The U.S. firm has begun suits against the Japanese company for selling its product in foreign markets where the U.S. firm holds patent rights. The U.S. firm has had some favorable rulings supporting its case. However, the U.S. company does not believe this is an effective remedy for protecting its technological competitiveness.

The U.S. firm also concluded that despite NTT's recent willingness to open bidding on telecommunications products to foreign firms, it has systematically used the refusal to patent new products to deny entry into Japan while using a protected home market to develop a competitive product similar to that produced in the United States. The U.S. company has reached this conclusion because, during the late 1970s, NTT was paying Japanese firms more to manufacture the product than it would have cost to buy it from the U.S. firm. Thus, the Japanese price was subsidizing product development by Japanese firms.

Subsequently, Japanese companies started to market this product in slightly different form in the United States for 30 percent under the market price. As a result, the United States firm has now lost sales in the U.S. market and is using several legal avenues to gain restitution.

In a similar case, a U.S. biotechnology firm found it was difficult to sell its products in France because of product testing restrictions being proposed by a number of agencies in the French government that will make organizing a distribution network in France very cumbersome. It has hesitated to proceed with licensing arrangements because its licensee cannot establish a stable distribution network because of possible testing bottlenecks. It may wait to see if another, larger firm will take over its marketing.

The restrictions that were likely to be imposed by the French government would check for the safety and performance of diagnostic products. The entry of non-French biotechnology products into the French market was likely to be limited by such testing, not because of any failure to conform to French standards, but because the testing limits the timeliness with which the French licensee could supply its customers with products they require.

The testing really constitutes a barrier to establishing the distribution network required to market a new product. The French licensee of the U.S. firm has found that the new regulations would make it extremely difficult to set up a distribution system. Without being able to guarantee a timely flow of products to distributors, the licensee cannot get enough firms to sign up to establish a distribution network for the U.S. firm. The U.S. firm has not pursued a way to sell in France, but is considering trying to get a large multinational firm to take over its foreign marketing because it could deal with such marketing problems more effectively.

III. Impacts on Investment

There were a number of cases where the location of investment was determined by market access requirements. In one well-known case, a U.S. semiconductor manufacturer was forced to invest in Japan to obtain access to local makets. In another case, standards and the approval of communications links could be used by European nations to bar firms from entering markets unless they were willing to provide local firms with an innovative technology.

In the latter case, a small U.S. telecommunications firm faced substantial difficulty in establishing itself in Germany. This was due to two problems related to standards. First, the German Bundespost would not give the firm frequency clearance for a downlink into Germany, that would enable it to provide data services in Germany that were transmitted from a computer in the United States via a direct broadcast satellite or a packet-switched network. Second, the German government would not approve the data base the U.S. firm wanted to provide because of concerns about the export of sensitive data about the German economy.

The firm faced these barriers in spite of the fact that it offered a service that no one in Germany was offering. It felt that there was great interest in seeing how it had managed to set up its system and was able to provide customers in Germany with everything from block mode or teletype (rather unsophisticated services) to an SNA gateway (a very sophisticated data gateway).

The firm felt that the German government was on a fishing expedition, using standards to get the U.S. firm to team up with a German firm and then to have the U.S. firm teach the German company what it was doing. The German government, however, wanted the U.S. firm to put up all the capital and did not want to buy any of the R&D that the firm had already done in order to compensate it for its expenses.

The U.S. firm spoke to several German companies about such an arrangement and approached them about establishing a joint venture. Nevertheless, when it drew up the memorandum of understanding (MOU) necessary to incorporate, the German firms were unwilling to provide any commitments of capital. The U.S. firm felt that even with a successful joint venture in place, it would have had no guarantee of access to the market.

The firm then approached the German Bundespost. An executive spoke with the head of the telecommunications policy section, recounting the barriers his firm faced. The representative of the Bundespost spoke with the potential joint-venture partners the U.S. firm had seen. Executives from these German firms then became resentful that the American executive had approached the government.

Because this U.S. firm can maximize its profits by expanding the use of the services it has designed, in order to get the R&D dollars invested in the product returned, standards and government requirements are key determinants of the firm's overall performance. Because standards such as those imposed by Germany forbid the firm from deploying a data base service without substantial modifications, and made it undertake major efforts to find a local partner, the firm's cost of business became too high and it could not operate in Germany.

It should also be noted that the firm had spent a considerable amount of time and funds before it sought to enter the German market developing a way to get around European standards that are incompatible with those established by the United States for satellite transmission. The United States uses 56 kilobit bandwidths, while the Europeans use 50 kilobits. This means there is a built-in incompatibility between U.S. and European systems at the physical interface level. The U.S. firm had to design new protocols to overcome this incompatibility.

Although it succeeded on a technical level, it was unable to convert its technical innovation into profits because of the pressure from the German government. Thus, standards can be linked with other NTBs, such as the need to approve a downlink and pressure to provide local firms with access to proprietary technology, to create an impossible situation for U.S. firms. This is especially true for smaller firms without local representatives who know how to get around the host government's regulations and how to utilize assistance from the U.S. government.

In addition, the firm's executives felt that the two years they had spent in developing the access technologies that permitted them to offer such a data base service in Europe had been wasted. They decided to refocus their efforts on the United States and Canada.

We were unable to find evidence of problems created when countries required U.S. investors to place a plant in an economically depressed region.

B. Investment Characteristics

Firms in the telecommunications industry also provided us with some of the best examples of how barriers affect investment decisions by U.S. firms. In one case, a major American electronics manufacturer maintains a small manufacturing and marketing presence in Brazil. This firm produces finished products in Brazil of a relatively low technology content. It also manufactures sophisticated systems of a high technology content in the United States, as well as parts and components for a variety of product lines. Some of these parts and components are required for the production of the low-end equipment produced in Brazil.

The Brazilian informatics market is monitored by the government's Special Secretariat of Informatics (SEI), which in 1979 assumed responsibilities for the data processing, microelectronics, telematics and real-time control systems industries. Since then SEI's strategy has been to enhance the capabilities of national corporations in manufacturing complex technologies. SEI encourages foreign affiliates to produce state-of-the-art computer goods and services in Brazil (both for local consumption and export), as well as to construct and improve local R&D facilities. Once a product line can be manufactured with local capital, the market is protected to give the infant industry an opportunity to develop. Foreign producers, who may have initially brought this technology into Brazil, are encouraged to move into more sophisticated products. Further development of the original product line is thus left to Brazilian manufacturers. As a result of this, imports are monitored through a licensing regime which enables the government to reduce or stem the flow of foreign-produced parts and components into the country once a local manufacturing capacity is developed.

This American company has not been successful in obtaining import licenses in Brazil for its sophisticated systems, and over the past eighteen to thirty-six months has faced delays in obtaining licenses both for parts and components and for finished products of a low technology content. The Brazilian government has informally intimated that import licenses for both low- and high-tech systems could be more readily obtained by this company if it were to develop local manufacturing capacity for the more sophisticated systems, and perhaps conduct greater levels of R&D in the country. Apparently the government presently believes that this company's current production, at the low end of the technology scale, does not significantly add to the productive base of Brazil's informatics industry, does not significantly add to export volume, and does not substantially contribute to the Brazilian efforts to build a local industry.

Although it is not certain, it appears that the two American market giants in Brazil, IBM and Burroughs, have been successful at obtaining import licenses for their equipment and parts in recent years. Together these two control a sizeable share of the Brazilian market and employ several thousand workers. Moreover, roughly eight years ago the Brazilian government attempted to deny import licenses to IBM. The resulting bottlenecks and shortages almost brought the automated capacity of the country--and the government--to a standstill. IBM was quickly reissued licenses.

Delays and difficulties in receiving import licenses for the parts and components necessary to produce low-technology equipment have led this company to scale back operations in Brazil. Generally the delays stemmed from an apparently arbitrary determination by the Brazilian bureaucracy as to whether licenses will be issued. The company was unable to explain why some licenses are denied, while others are granted soon thereafter. The difficulties arise from the financial arrangements stipulated by the Brazilian government. Currency restrictions are imposed, and the company is required to hold cruzeiros (the local currency) for extended periods at a time of high inflation. Moreover, given the present financial difficulties of the country, there is no guarantee that the cruzeiros will indeed be exchanged for dollars. As a result of these and other problems, the company is steadily reducing production and employment in its local operations. The Brazilian government has not, up to the present, shown any willingness to ease its terms and issue the range and number of import licenses necessary for a profitable and growing business for this company in Brazil.

In another case (described earlier under Investment Location), a small U.S. telecommunications firm withdrew from Germany rather than license its innovative data base system to a local firm, which would have involved little or no compensation for its research and development cost and important design breakthrough. The firm had developed an information system that it believed was both competitive and unique. The high costs associated with the development of the system--which required two years--were financed through retained earnings. The significant level of resources this firm has devoted to this information system reflects its belief that the market potential is extraordinary. As do most small firms in this industry, it saw the greatest potential for market growth and development abroad, and recently attempted to market the system in West Germany.

In providing the information system to German users, this company wanted to retain central processing facilities in the United States to use some of the available technology here (such as international packet switching and direct broadcast satellite capabilities). The U.S. firm made clear that it could be flexible, and that it would adapt to whichever satellite downlink frequency the federal government felt appropriate. Yet the German authorities stalled in authorizing the company's use of a downlink frequency necessary for communications.

It soon became clear that the German government was reluctant to allow the deployment of an information-based system that enabled German terminals to access remote data bases outside the country. This U.S. firm, however, was unable to ascertain what kind of information the government considered to be sensitive. The particular application for this project was a financial-based system that conducted simple debit checking. As a result of the German government's reluctance, it appeared that this firm would not be able to implement the service as designed.

The government did informally suggest two German companies that might license the American firm's technology and become the firm's local representative. Many of the problems facing this firm, it was implied, might be eased if this course were chosen. Local representation frequently is secured by larger firms through, for example, wholly owned subsidiaries or simply local offices that enable these companies to better anticipate changes in their markets. Local connections also are highly effective in easing the effects of NTBs once they appear. This particular firm, however, was too small to afford such local representation, and a joint venture through a technology licensing arrangement appeared to be the only alternative. Yet the two German companies suggested by government officials refused to commit themselves financially. These German firms, recognizing the difficulties their American counterpart was having in breaking into the German market, offered only their marketing facilities in exchange for training in, and access to, the technologies developed in the United States. Moreover, there were no assurances for the American firm that further nontariff barriers would not soon appear to block market access once the technology had been transferred to the German companies.

But most importantly, this American firm was reluctant to transfer that know-how that had been developed in-house at considerable expense. Much of the significant technological developments taking place in the telecommunications industry are carried out in smaller, innovative firms such as this one. They view the successful exploitation of these developments into products or services as key to their survival. Yet, oftentimes their companies find it difficult to both market a product abroad and control the relevant technology. The alternative to the licensing of the technology, and the path chosen here, was to quit the German market entirely and settle for the American and Canadian markets. The growth potential is not as great, but without local representation in the German market, it does not appear feasible for this company to provide services there.

There was not much evidence disclosed in this study about whether employment requirements and local sourcing regulations were important causes of increased costs for U.S. firms.

IV. Impacts on Exporting

Buy-national policies, rather than arbitrary customs difficulties or certification rulings, had the greatest impact on U.S. firms we studied. In one case, a U.S. earth station equipment company was informed by the Japanese government that procurement by NTT, the main Japanese telephone company, would be liberalized as a result of negotiations with the United States. A major project was being initiated by NTT for a development program that was expected to last five years or more. The program was for the construction of earth station equipment using very large scale integrated circuits (VLSI) products developed through an earlier government-sponsored program. The U.S. firm was eager to participate because entry into the program meant not only sales to the Japanese market but also an opportunity to learn some of the production techniques developed in Japan to use large-scale integrated circuits from the VLSI program.

The U.S. firm was advised that two contracts would be awarded by NTT for the development program, one to a Japanese firm and one to an American firm. The U.S. firm thought it had an excellent chance to win a contract because it was extremely competitive with the Japanese companies it faced in world markets and very much on the technological forefront of the industry. However, the price it bid on the contract was--according to NTT--considerably higher than that bid by NEC and by another Japanese firm. As a consequence, the two contracts were awarded to the two Japanese companies, in spite of the fact that the U.S. firm had been informed before the bidding was opened that one Japanese and one U.S. firm would be selected as contractors.

The U.S. company that bid on the contract believes it was misled. It is now much more reluctant to try to enter the Japanese market. Since it now has a market in the rest of the world that is much more lucrative, it has focused its energies on these non-Japanese, foreign opportunities. The firm, however, was especially disappointed because it competes with NEC on international tenders and wins its share. In other foreign markets, it has not had problems with its price being higher than that of NEC. The U.S. firm feels that there may have been some special arrangements that enabled NEC to come up with a very low bid in Japan.

Representatives of the U.S. firm also feel that the Japanese did not want to let the U.S. company into Japan's market. Historically, NTT has worked very closely with NEC. The U.S. firm's executives had the feeling that NEC was very unhappy about two contracts being offered by NTT, especially because one was expected to go to a foreign competitor. The U.S. firm's staff surmised that because of NEC's concern, it had exerted considerable political pressure on the Japanese government and on NTT in order to have the contracts given to two Japanese firms. Although none of the U.S. firm's executives wanted to argue that the prices bid on the contract were linked to a desire to keep only Japanese firms in the bidding, there was an insinuation that things were very different in bidding for the Japanese market and in bidding for markets outside of Japan. The lower prices bid by Japanese firms for the Japanese contract were seen as related to a political strategy of wanting to keep non-Japanese firms from playing an active role in the development of new technologies. The fear motivating Japanese firms to act in this way, as it was perceived by U.S. executives, was that there might be an opportunity for non-Japanese firms to devise unique ways to adapt Japanese technologies that would give Japan's competitors advantages in international markets and in Japan's own market before Japanese firms had adequate time to develop similar products or other innovative products that would provide them with niches in critical markets. Thus, NTBs were seen as playing an important protective role, locking out the competition and giving Japanese firms more opportunity to exploit their own technological innovations.

In this case, the Japanese approach is very different from that taken by many U.S. firms. Historically, U.S. companies have been very eager to license new technologies very soon after they were proved to be commercially viable and to earn income from these innovations by letting foreign firms sell products based on such innovations. This may have grown out of a fear that short product life cycles in high-technology areas would reduce the opportunity for profit-making. However, another risk is involved with high-technology products. This risk is that licensees will be able to copy and adapt the product for their own markets and even for the markets of the licensor. This has, in fact, been the case with the U.S. color TV industry and also with U.S. semiconductor manufacturers, where licensing of state-of-the-art technology to the Japanese led to a rapid closing of technological gaps and, in the case of color TVs, an overtaking of U.S. firms. In software, however, U.S. firms have begun to behave differently and are often very reluctant to license state-of-the-art software to foreign firms, fearing they will lose control over the evolution of their product. This change of heart on licensing by firms in some of the newer high-technology industries may indicate that U.S. firms now recognize the real importance of controlling innovative technologies until they can achieve an important market position that is based upon their early introduction and continued ownership of new products. NTBs are one mechanism that can be used to assure such control, and discouraging foreign firms from entering key markets, such as those in Japan, through national firm-oriented procurement practices, is one way to promote indigenous development of what are considered critical technologies.

Another factor that may result in this type of behavior is the Japanese fear that strong U.S. firms will move rapidly to take over parts of the Japanese market if the pace of entry is not controlled. NTBs appear to serve as a means to control the pace of deregulation of the telecommunications market in Japan, in part because it is difficult to predict how the shift to more competitive procurement policies will affect the competitiveness of Japanese companies. To protect some of the larger firms against the impacts of deregulation, NTBs in areas such as procurement may be slow in coming down.

The lack of type certification, as mentioned in the case of the U.S. computer and communications equipment manufacturer presented above, also can result in decreased export competitiveness for U.S. firms.

In another case, we found that the government-assisted financing provided by some European nations discouraged U.S. high-technology firms from competing for exports. We spoke to a small U.S. software firm that often bids on government RFPs for Western European nations. In many of these cases, it faces important national firms in the computer and computer services industry, such as Thomson-CSF or CIT-Alcatel, when turnkey combinations of hardware and software are requested.

The U.S. firm develops customized software to meet the specialized requirements of domestic and foreign corporations. It has found that when it attempts to compete with some of the larger European computer manufacturers that are also important providers of this type of turnkey equipment, it is extremely difficult to win important contracts. This happens because the European firms, especially those from France, are able to go to their governments and obtain cheap, long-term financing for the firms that want to purchase such turnkey systems. This has often been done at the very last moment, literally pulling the rug out from under the deals that the U.S. firms felt were wrapped up.

As a consequence, the U.S. firm is now very careful when it enters into competition against European firms for such turnkey systems. It often asks prospective buyers which other companies they are asking for bids. If the French firms are involved, the U.S. firm is likely to shy away from taking part in the competition for the sales because it does not want to waste staff time and travel and development money trying to make the sale, only to find that one of the French companies has come in with extremely low-cost, long-term government-assisted financing.

This occurs in spite of the fact that the software provided by the U.S. firm for the turnkey system is definitely a more sophisticated solution for the user, with a lower operating cost. Nevertheless, because of the government-assisted financing obtained by the French firms, the French competitors can argue that they are removing 5 to 6 percent from the total cost of the project by not forcing the purchaser to use market financing.

The U.S. firm feels that the French firms can use government-assisted financing in a very targeted manner. The executive who described this case depicted the French company as going back to the French government and saying, "We need a little more oomph on this one." This concern is reinforced by the belief that this type of government-industry cooperation is very ingrained in the French system and can easily be put into motion, while support for U.S. exporters from Eximbank is much more limited and takes more time to mobilize, except in the case of major contracts.

In addition, this executive felt that his firm's experiences, losing contracts in the face of strong foreign government financial assistance, had an impact on its R&D spending. The firm did not want to allocate funds for projects it should compete for in Europe and other foreign markets. It feared that French firms could easily use government-backed financing to win contracts, even though the French software and turnkey systems were not as efficient and sophisticated as those provided by the U.S. company. It now feels there is no point in bidding on such contracts.

5
The Impact of Nontariff Barriers on U.S. Policy

INTRODUCTION

A cornerstone of the Tokyo Round negotiations was the achievement of several codes of conduct designed to limit national discretion in the imposition of nontariff barriers. A number of the distortions addressed by these codes--licensing, standards, and procurement--have been relieved somewhat, particularly over the last year. One recent example has been rulings by the Italian courts to publish government procurement needs, a step that has prodded other European governments to establish more open notification practices. The progress of U.S.-Japanese bilateral discussions in clarifying and simplifying Japanese standards practices, reducing procurement discrimination in telecommunications, and opening up Japanese government-funded R&D projects for U.S. participation is also noteworthy.

At the same time, however, roadblocks still exist that are slowing the removal of barriers. Despite NTT's commitment to a more open procurement policy, a number of U.S. companies have been thwarted in their efforts to sell to NTT because the time permitted for bidding is very short. In the EEC, policies developed in the Community's confrontation with IBM may result in more NTBs, rather than fewer. A number of nations are carefully watching Brazil's policies toward the information industries, worried that Brazil's independent path may serve as a model for other nations.

All of these problems raise concerns for corporate government relations staffs and for government agencies that are interested in improving the competitiveness of U.S. high-technology firms. Foreign markets are critical for assuring the rapid and profitable commercialization of new, high-technology products. Barriers to these markets restrict corporations' flexibility and may reduce their innovative capacity and desire to compete vigorously for international sales. A more domestic focus may not hinder the rapid expansion of some high-technology companies. Nevertheless, an international presence has become invaluable for corporate stability and growth as a number of the more successful U.S. firms such as IBM have demonstrated. Withdrawal from international markets also may have significant long-term consequences for the U.S. economy.

QUESTIONS CONCERNING THE IMPACT OF NTBs ON U.S. POLICY

Starting from this brief overview, there is a range of key questions that deserve attention by policymakers and negotiators. They suggest areas in which governments' reaction to NTBs might be improved.

I. Current Policy Issues

A. Problems in Enforcing the Tokyo Round Reductions of NTBs

1. What special problems are associated with the monitoring of NTB code enforcement? Technical nature of the barrier? Complexity of foreign government bureaucracies? Ambiguities of the codes? Inadequate contacts with industry? Disinterest of U.S. embassies?
2. Which high-tech industries face the biggest problems here?
3. What is the best approach for the government to use to improve compliance with these codes?
4. What can the private sector contribute to improve compliance?

B. Government-Industry Relations

1. An American company's agreement to conduct R&D and/or investment abroad may be in response to an NTB conditioning access to a foreign market. While this could run counter to American policy objectives in these industries, the appropriate government agencies may be unaware of the NTB or agreement stemming from it. Is the implementation of American trade, investment, and R&D policy objectives significantly inhibited by a lack of close company consultation with the U.S. government on barriers in foreign markets?

2. What characteristics of the U.S. trade agencies discourage American companies with trade-related problems from using U.S. agencies to resolve such problems?

    a. Individual companies often seek to use NTBs in foreign markets to their advantage over competing firms.
    b. Company fear of retaliation from the local government for initiating an official complaint discourages the use of government offices.
    c. Companies may view government intervention as too time consuming or creating additional difficulties.

3. Through what means can U.S. trade policy officials obtain better information on corporate reactions to foreign barriers on a case-by-case basis, such as technology licensing or local investment arrangements? Is greater government anticipation and initiative possible?
4. In some instances, corporations rely on their own experts to reduce the impact of NTBs on their efforts to enter foreign markets. This approach is particularly common to large U.S. high-tech firms. How significant are the disadvantages that this creates for other, smaller U.S. firms that do not have the ability to negotiate with foreign governments? Do many smaller U.S. firms opt out of exporting because of their small staffing resources and the foreign regulatory complexities involved?
5. Can these disadvantages to smaller manufacturers be addressed by government policymakers?
6. At hearings last fall over the renewal of the NTT procurement agreement, most of the American telecommunications companies offering testimony supported the renewal (which many in government did not). The marked lack of official Japanese purchases after three years of trading under the original agreement was explained by these companies as due to cultural factors in the Japanese market that require at least this much time to overcome. Given that many NTBs are based on, or exacerbated by, cultural factors, is it inappropriate for these to be addressed through government offices?

II. New Areas for Government Policy

A. Has the development of new and increasingly complex technologies led to a change in the institutional responsibility for addressing NTBs concerning these technologies, resulting in a shift of oversight from government to industry, and from the trade agencies to more technical agencies (FAA, FTC, NASA, DOD, OSTP, etc.)?

1. Government agencies may lack the expertise necessary to address these complex issues effectively.
2. If responsibility shifted to industry, this would enable foreign governments to play companies off among one another.

B. Can the deregulation of U.S. industries and the likelihood that significant NTBs will be removed at home without reciprocal moves abroad be structured so that the impacts that deregulation will have on the international competitiveness of U.S. high-tech firms are taken into account?

1. New legislation introduced by Senator Danforth and others for the telecommunications sector addresses the fact that the deregulation of the U.S. telephone industry by judicial ruling (Judge Green's decision) has removed many domestic NTBs (e.g., the integration of operating companies and Western Electric in AT&T) without any agreement from foreign PTTs to open their markets. This may improve efforts to remove NTBs both at home and abroad.

C. Will there be a spillover effect as foreign companies gain footholds in the U.S. telecommunications market (after deregulation) and are thereby better positioned to move into related high-technology areas?

D. Possible changes in the approach that foreign governments take to U.S. firms operating in their markets may result in additional NTBs. Likely hotspots include the EEC (where IBM has experienced repeated difficulties due to EEC wishes to improve the competitive environment for its own information industries) and Brazil (where U.S. firms have encountered numerous barriers designed to transfer technology, investment, and R&D to local firms). What government policies could be adopted to cope with these anticipated changes?

E. Is progress to limit such problems likely only at GATT negotiations or could bilateral negotiations prove useful? Is the U.S.-Japan dialogue a model for future bilaterals with individual European countries, the NICs, and so forth?

F. Are new joint business-government initiatives in this area appropriate to these changing markets?

G. NTBs will likely be an important subject for future ministerial meetings on trade problems. The agenda for these meetings is normally developed far in advance--often several years--and the role of NTBs in future negotiations should be addressed now. What NTBs should be central to the U.S. negotiating agenda?

H. What informational or background materials should be developed in preparing for negotiations? Specifically, would an updated inventory of nontariff barriers provide necessary background information? Would some quantification of their effects be credible and useful?

I. NTBs are not simply market protecting, border measures in the classic sense (as are tariffs and quotas); they are key instruments of domestic industrial and technology policies designed to enhance global competitiveness. As such, they are designed to have a specific promotional effect on targeted industries. Do these links between the NTB regime and the development priorities of governments have implications for U.S. trade policy and our government's information base? Do they make NTBs more intractable? Do they diffuse responsibility within the offending government? Do they suggest the need for sectoral agreements embodying some concept of reciprocity? Do they require greater knowledge of emerging technologies among the trade agencies?

J. Are the ultimate consequences of such practices important as trade policy issues, assuming they result in enhanced competitiveness and losses of market shares for U.S. firms? If they are, how can these longer-term considerations be reconciled with the short-term, firm-specific calculations of U.S. companies that may dictate cooperation with foreign NTBs?

K. One of the unique characteristics of trade negotiations in high-technology sectors (aside from the R&D intensity of the industries themselves and the special instruments of import protection imposed) involves a close link between technology policy and national security. This link has if anything been strengthened by the enlarged role of the U.S. Defense Department in reviewing high-technology export license applications for trade with other OECD countries (from which diversions may occur to controlled areas). This has compromised the credibility of U.S. high-technology trade negotiators, who seek access to high-technology markets abroad while foreign country access to U.S. technology is being restricted. What strategies--both internal bureaucratic and diplomatic--are available to the trade agencies to reestablish a consistent and reciprocal U.S. commitment to free trade in high-technology products and reinforce U.S. leverage at likely multilateral negotiations next year?

PROBLEMS IN ENFORCING THE TOKYO ROUND REDUCTIONS OF NTBs

During our panel of trade policymakers and Washington representatives of U.S. firms, concern was expressed by a number of panelists that foreign governments were much more sophisticated in their use of NTBs, particularly since the reduction in tariffs achieved in the Tokyo Round negotiations left NTBs as the main trade policy device to use in promoting high-technology industries. This concern was coupled with a recognition that many U.S. high-technology firms were not very sophisticated when it came to confronting NTBs and in recognizing their impact on the growth of their own business overseas.

A number of participants felt that not enough had been done to improve the way NTBs were removed. When Japan liberalized its telecommunications industry, there were no performance criteria established in the agreements reached by the U.S. Trade Representative with the government of Japan. However, a number of participants felt that the pressure in Europe to achieve more competitive high-tech industries would alleviate a number of the NTBs that had proved troublesome to U.S. firms.

On the other hand, several participants felt that the Europeans had become even more sophisticated in their use of incompatible standards to make it harder for U.S. firms to penetrate the EEC's markets, particularly in telecommunications. These panelists were concerned about the large size of several new telecommunications innovations that are about to be put in place over the next decade. These could be more affected by NTBs than something like a biotechnology system. In some cases, although U.S. products were more efficient, they could be excluded if they failed to conform to special European standards.

Several approaches to NTBs were suggested by the panelists. One was to let industry groups take over the U.S. response. Another was to create a sort of early-warning system in the government to initiate the dissemination of information about new NTBs that could harm U.S. firms. A third approach was to try to establish a global framework for the removal of NTBs.

Some participants also believed that the roadblocks that hindered U.S. government action could be exacerbated by the shortening of the product life cycle for high-technology products. This makes government oversight more difficult and may increase the problems industry faces in determining the impact of NTBs.

Some approaches that were suggested to remove the roadblocks included: undertaking bilateral negotiations to remove the most troublesome NTBs, promoting direct industry-to-industry discussions when government initiatives seem inappropriate, and improving the bargaining capacity of U.S. negotiators by expanding the range of domestic remedies to targeted high-technology exports of our competitors.

GOVERNMENT-INDUSTRY RELATIONS

Government-Industry Interactions

One participant argued that the French were very interested in cooperating in improving entrepreneurship and innovation in their high-technology industries. They want to allow U.S. firms to make good deals and have access to their market, to help meet the main French goals to increase industrial and academic collaboration and to improve competitiveness, through help from U.S. high-technology firms. This participant believed that such collaboration would not risk an erosion of U.S. leadership, since firms in emerging high-technology sectors would--unlike semiconductor firms in the 1970s--be moving into new generations of technology very rapidly.

Several government officials feared that such a sanguine view of NTBs would lead to a repeat of the problems faced by U.S. semiconductor manufacturers in the early 1970s. Lack of sophistication led them to believe the Japanese were willing to cooperate in developing new technology. Most executives failed to recognize how much Japanese NTBs that closed the Japanese market to U.S. firms would affect their development. Such controlled access to the Japanese market was seen as a major reason why U.S. firms now face stiff competition from the Japanese. Safely behind a protected border, the Japanese firms, aided by targeting policies of their government, could develop their own products and profit from an often artificially stimulated indigenous demand under oligopolistic conditions. This facilitated an extension of the reach of these Japanese firms into the world marketplace.

This argument was supported by some government officials who warned that the situation is very different today from the 1970s. Foreign governments are now much more sophisticated in the use of NTBs. There are fewer tariffs and different criteria for NTBs. Patent filing problems have become more of a barrier. The Japanese are more sophisticated because they now use foreign investment in the United States to acquire access to emerging high-technology firms, largely cash-poor, venture-type firms from which they can license technology and transfer it to Japan more readily. For U.S. firms, one problem with the latter approach is that in Japan, large firms with substantial resources do much of the development and commercialization of high-technology products, while in the United States, small firms still are responsible for a sizeable part of these costs in high technology.

U.S. government officials now face problems because no clear constituency exists in some high-tech industries to support government initiatives to remove NTBs. In addition, even when government plays a role intended to spark industry activisim, firms often break ranks to strike their own deals with foreign governments. This can result in some larger or more influential firms establishing terms that protect their own interests to the detriment of others. Sometimes these deals can turn out to be albatrosses for companies that are not sophisticated enough to understand the inner workings of overseas markets. This has occurred when acquisitions by U.S. firms give them a role in companies in industries that are being squeezed by the host government.

On the other hand, one government observer argued that NTBs can be used to develop access to the U.S. market. A government, such as Japan's, can weaken NTBs to facilitate a U.S. firm's entry into its market, but can then use such a move toward more liberal trade policy to argue for greater access by Japanese firms to U.S. markets. This hidden agenda can provide a very meaningful way for Japanese firms to gain better access to new technology and to obtain a greater number of outlets for their own products.

The Scope for Government Action and Rival Government Industrial Policies

Some U.S. officials believe that government has been ahead of industry in identifying NTBs. But companies also feel frustrated with the government's lack of results. These very different interpretations of the role played by government seem to be tied to how one interprets trade theory. If one believes that comparative advantage will always win in the end, even when subsidies are employed by one government and not another, there is less likelihood one will be very concerned about NTBs. If, however, one is not convinced that competitiveness is driven largely by comparative advantage, but instead, believes that government subsidies or trade barriers can bring about shifts in competitiveness, a different approach to NTBs is required. One problem arising from this wide difference in orientation is that it obscures the approach the government should take toward policy in this area.

At the present time, most policymakers in Washington believe that comparative advantage determines competitiveness. Even accepting this, there are still important questions about what levels of pain can be accepted in terms of industrial distress that can be accommodated by U.S. firms. There is also the question of how NTBs and the trade strategies of our trading partners affect their role in negotiations. If others have a different objective in trade negotiations, perhaps U.S. policymakers should be thinking about achieving strategic trade advantages rather than focusing on free trade.

There is also the problem of who are the constituents of the government. Multinational corporations have more ability to grandfather arrangements with host governments. Other firms have less ability to cut deals with foreign nations. In addition, there is the question of just how the government goes about motivating firms to become more aware of trade policy problems. It has tried to educate firms, to do competitive assessments and to address industry groups. But its hands are often tied if there is a lack of unanimity among the firms in the industry.

Concern over how smaller firms could cope with NTBs was voiced by several participants. It was generally agreed that trade associations played an important role in improving information flow and exchange that was especially helpful to small firms. On the other hand, the lack of focus of U.S. policy goals was seen as a hindrance to smaller firms coping adequately with NTBs.

Remedies

Some remedies were suggested for the problems created in the past by ineffective government-industry relations in the face of NTBs. One is to have greater coordination of industry-level activity under the supervision of the private sector rather than the government. Another is to have the U.S. government initiate critical information dissemination to warn firms of impending changes in NTBs that will have a major impact on their business. A third opinion claimed that perceptions and policy lag reality; that U.S. policy should continue to focus on the twin goals of promoting greater trade while at the same time seeking further liberalization of trade barriers through GATT.

THE NEED FOR BETTER DATA

The need for better information has often made it difficult for government trade policy officials to assist corporations in reacting to foreign NTBs. An initial goal of this project was to develop a compendium of nontariff barriers using existing data sources. This was ambitious, but it appeared that by using sources in GATT, the U.S. Trade Representative's Office, the Office of Import Administration at Commerce, and trade associations, it would be possible to compile a guide to NTBs. Nevertheless, once these sources were examined in greater detail, we found a number of significant shortcomings in them that undermined our ability to prepare a useful compendium. First, few of the compilations had been kept up to date. In the case of the STR's data, although NTBs in services have been followed closely and are documented in some detail by form, applicable nation and sectoral coverage, STR's more general NTB data base ("Non-Tariff Barrier Analysis") is very out of date and not provided in a great deal of detail. In 1977, the Department of Commerce became responsible for a subsequent version, "Non-Tariff Barriers." This was updated through April 1981, in preparation for the GATT Ministerial in November of that year. It has not been updated since, except in isolated cases. Moreover, a cursory inspection of it would suggest that old NTBs were not consistently edited out in the update process.

There are several sources of information on NTBs that are incomplete. The official GATT inventory (which is separate from the inventory maintained through 1981 by the Department of Commerce), for example, is based on government notifications and is therefore by definition a partial accounting (political considerations may preclude a formal notification against another country). The UNCTAD data base focuses on North-South trade. The OECD study on trade barriers in high-technology sectors is in its infancy and has been severely crippled by a lack of full OECD country cooperation. The Office of the European Community within the International Trade Administration of the Department of Commerce has updated its listing of the "Non-Tariff Barriers" data base--although the revision does not appear to be thorough. The USTR now maintains an inventory of barriers to investment, and another listing of barriers to services is presently being compiled. Moreover, the Foreign Trade Action Monitoring Service, maintained by USTR, addresses some NTBs in its coverage of all current trade disputes. But taken together, the coverage is spotty and inconsistent and does not provide a coherent picture of the situation.

Consequently, the preparation of better data would improve the ability of trade officials to assist U.S. companies. Although we spent some time searching for other inventories of nontariff barriers and attempted to use a more recent data base compiled by the United Nations Conference on Trade and Development, we met with little success. We concluded that a substantial amount of time would need to be devoted to the preparation of an up-to-date and comprehensive compendium; most of those available are still two years out of date, fail to focus on high-technology sectors, and may include NTBs that were already negotiated away. (See Appendix A on data sources.)

NTBs AND THE PROMOTION OF HIGH-TECHNOLOGY INDUSTRIES BY FOREIGN GOVERNMENTS

A crucial factor promoting the growth of NTBs has been the desire by foreign governments to promote the growth of indigenous high-technology industries. Many nations seek to emulate Japan's success in the 1970s, particularly the European countries undergoing dynamic changes in their industrial structure.

This pressure has already led to a number of developments that are likely to increase the importance of NTBs as a policy issue. Among the most notable are the initiatives in the EEC to develop incompatible standards.

The EEC is now developing its own standards, especially in telecommunications. While there is an effort to get more participation in European markets by large U.S. high-technology firms such as IBM and AT&T, there is a clear tendency to establish policies to suit a technical standard such as X.25 and ISDN. A large, fixed telecommunications system, such as ISDN, may be more controllable and affected by NTBs than a biotechnology system.

European economies are likely to face great pressure over the next few years to get away from their balkanization in order to become more competitive. While this would meet U.S. firms' desires to have a harmonization of standards within Europe, based largely on the standards code, it will also erode the monopoly position of the European PTTs. This could lead the Europeans to rely more heavily on unique standards for their own EEC market, establishing a unique set of policy objectives in setting up its NTBs. It would be difficult to reconcile these goals with those of U.S. industry or government policymakers, especially if they were adjusted to contend with emerging technologies. It also would be difficult to penetrate the old boys' networks and to counter country--or EEC--designated favorites in foreign markets without a substantial change in the attitude of the business communities in foreign countries.

OPPORTUNITIES FOR NEW INITIATIVES TO REDUCE THE USE OF NTBs

Industry representatives have argued that not much had been achieved in trade negotiations to remove NTBs. In telecommunications, the Japanese have been slow to liberalize procurement for their phone system, even after they had formally agreed to do so. It was felt that this reflected a failure to include performance criteria in the agreements reached by the USTR and too much of an emphasis on procedures. There also is frustration directed at the U.S. government for the way it has handled relations with Japan, problems in software valuation and procurement, and disagreements over arrangements with industrialized versus developing nations.

It was felt the U.S. government should adopt accords on new standards that require specific changes in performance. Another participant argued that the standards issue is complex because it encompasses broader issues of discriminatory access to the certification of systems and acceptance of test results that require some tie to a broader policy toward NTBs. This is the case with software, where U.S. firms may be unable to compete due to their lack of compatibility with standards.

Some observers argued that if NTBs are removed, U.S. firms that are very strong in a technological sense can enter new markets and sell their products successfully. The problem is that, in some cases such as telecommunications, deregulation results in increased competition and makes successful market entry by U.S. firms more difficult. Thus, a similar approach to the one taken for auto industry negotiations in Latin America could be more successful because it would set goals that are congruent with the aims of specific U.S. high-technology industries and seek to trade off access to U.S. markets for better entry into foreign ones.

This may, however, require an industry consensus, a consensus among government agencies, and political leverage. Whether such a consensus for negotiations might be developed in the process of pursuing the negotiations themselves, as was the case in the Tokyo Round, is unclear. Government policymakers at the panel emphasized how difficult it was for them to initiate negotiations because some U.S. firms would not support talks to remove NTBs and because few trade associations focused attention on NTBs in high-technology areas.

THE NEED FOR AN EARLY-WARNING MECHANISM

Policymakers were concerned about how to develop a way to respond to NTBs before their detrimental impacts became too widespread. In semiconductors, one pointed out, the problem had come and gone. Today's question is how to stretch out the process of oversight, how to view the problem. This is difficult since it is often very hard to assess the impacts of NTBs on the marketplace. Responding to NTBs also may be more difficult in the case of high-technology industries because there is not much appreciation of the fact that NTBs can have a big impact on these industries.

Another participant noted the disincentives that existed for the government to play a role in the removal of NTBs facing high-technology industries. First, it is difficult for the government to oversee what was happening because NTBs can change rapidly and there are always pressures to license new technology. Second, the government does not really have capable analysts, primarily because these analysts have no real power and few incentives to remain in their posts, as demonstrated by the rapid turnover in staff at key government agencies.

To resolve these problems, it was suggested there be bilateral negotiations over the most troublesome NTBs. One participant noted this had been tried in several cases over the past two years and had a positive effect on the negotiations over software valuation. In a sense, the U.S. government is moving in this direction with the U.S.-Japan High Technology Working Group.

THE NEED FOR GREATER COMPATIBILITY OF STANDARDS AND PROCEDURES

Other initiatives that would be followed include having foreign countries accept testing done by U.S. firms in their U.S. facilities, especially where type acceptance is involved, and trying to establish interconnect procedures similar to those in force in the United States. In cases where an initiative by government has not been successful, as in Brazil, more direct industry-to-industry approaches ought to be considered. When U.S. industry representatives went to the U.S.-Brazilian Businessmen's Committee to discuss their concerns about the impact of Brazil's new telecommunications policy on U.S. firms selling to Brazil, they succeeded in obtaining changes where the U.S. government had failed.

Appendix A
Data Collection and Data Bases

PROBLEMS OF DATA COLLECTION

One of the difficulties confronted in a study on the policy impacts of nontariff barriers is that of collecting complete information, both from companies and government agencies. Aside from an occasional reluctance to discuss these issues at length, corporate representatives were often uncertain where, in their organization, most of the NTB-related information concerning their companies could be found. The excutives within the various companies we interviewed that are responsible for addressing nontariff barriers in foreign markets held very different positions, so it was not easy to identify where this expertise was developed. Aside from a lack of sufficient information among the government trade agencies in Washington, we found several obstacles in obtaining information from companies in doing the research for this project:

1. In small- and medium-sized firms, marketing managers may not be directly involved in international licensing arrangements. These may instead have been drawn up by a president or executive vice president.
2. Few companies estimate the costs of barriers or the additional work they may require; some may overestimate the impacts, others may minimize them.
3. In large companies, there is often great difficulty in identifying the specific individuals who are knowledgeable about the range of nontariff barriers that the company faces.
4. Larger firms often appear to be reluctant to talk about cases where they have made arrangements with foreign governments to overcome a nontariff barrier, or have successfully adjusted to the NTB through local manufacturing.

Our difficulties within the trade agencies in Washington were even greater. No listing of nontariff barriers has been updated since 1981. The Office of the European Community within the Department of Commerce independently updates the GATT nontariff barrier inventory, but as this is based on notifications, it is by definition incomplete. One exception to these omissions is the Inventory of Investment Barriers maintained by the Office of Investment Policy within USTR. This information, however, is very general. Additional problems in data collection that have arisen include:

- Within the trade agencies there is often an awareness of a problem, but as companies do not always report the NTBs they encounter, trade policy officials are not always aware of the details of the barrier nor of any efforts by the firm to circumvent it.
- Government trade officials are, by the nature of their work, often more concerned with violations of existing NTB codes and statutes than they are with NTBs that, while at times more significant than those addresssed by regulations, are not presently addressed by international statutes.

We sought suggestions from panelists in our study about how to improve information and data collection concerning NTBs. More specifically, we asked them:

- What can be done to reestablish NTB inventories such as those that were maintained in the 1970s?
- What can be done to improve company notification of NTBs to government?
- How can government trade offices responsible for maintaining information on NTBs be more readily identified, and how can these offices improve and expand their information to better help American businesses--particularly small ones--enter into export?

The panelists' opinions on how to improve data differed widely, but most agreed that NTBs should be studied in depth on a real-time basis. It also was suggested that a few policy issues be given priority for a more detailed evaluation, relying on interviews with the key U.S. firms involved and broadening the study group to include major users of high-technology products (Citibank in the case of telecommunications), in addition to producers.

There was general agreement that more attention should be paid to NTBs in the EEC and Korea, in order to respond better to problems that may arise as these nations attempt to employ NTBs to promote their high-technology sectors.

DATA BASES ON HIGH-TECHNOLOGY TRADE BARRIERS

The following data bases were examined in our attempt to develop a compendium of NTBs. Although this task was too vast to undertake, these data sources helped us identify NTBs and high-technology industries affected by NTBs that were the focus of our study.

1. UNCTAD Data Base on NTBs

Contents: "All governmental procedures and measures of a product-specific nature which have the potential to restrain or distort international trade flows"

Description: Four-digit Customs Cooperation Council Nomenclature (formerly known as BTN, Brussels Tariff Nomenclature) followed by the national tariff-line code

Available: Computer listings for selected high-tech, four-digit, categories. Others on request to UNCTAD, but last request took over six months to process

Contact: Andrew Olechowski
Manufactures Division
UNCTAD
Palais des Nations
CH 1211 Geneva 10
Switzerland

Report Generated: "Protectionism and Structural Adjustment: Non-Tariff Barriers Affecting the Trade of Developing Countries and Transparency in World Trading Conditions; The Inventory of Non-Tariff Barriers," TD/B/940, February 2, 1983

2. GATT NTB Inventory

Contents: Reports from countries themselves on NTBs or what one country has alleged about another's disposition of NTBs

Description: By country, providing type of NTB

Available: In eight or nine main documents, with five main sections and five addenda, each of which needs to be consulted to identify an NTB implemented by a specific nation

Restrictions: Only available to government officials because of government submissions

Now being updated and expanded

Based primarily on government notification, so that political considerations may have preceded formal notification of some NTBs

Contact: Dan Gardner
ITA/U.S. Dept. of Commerce
(202) 377-3681

3. GATT Quantitative Restrictions Inventory

Contents: The quantitative restrictions reported by GATT nations or alleged to be imposed by one nation reporting on another

Description: By product, listing quantitative restrictions. May include a reform dated compilation of the older GATT (requested by US DOC, but not approved as of 10/84)

Available: Currently being compiled (10/84)

Contact: Dan Gardner
ITA/U.S. Dept. of Commerce
(202) 377-3681

4. OECD Trade Barriers in High Technology

Contents:	Unclear at present (10/84), but likely to include a summary of government submissions to the OECD study on NTBs in high-tech sectors
Available:	Six sectoral studies that may be released shortly. These studies focus on nine trade problems. However, the studies are uneven in their coverage of national information
Contact:	Timothy Hauser U.S. Dept. of Commerce (202) 377-5853

5. STR Inventory of Investment Barriers

Contents:	Trade barriers for major trading partners, categorized largely in terms of import policies (quotas, customs, tariffs), regulatory policies (standards, testing, licensing), industrial policy (industry targeting, government procurement) and private-sector barriers such as distribution systems
Description:	Largely derived from reports on foreign government legislation and policies compiled by U.S. embassies. Varies greatly in detail and quality
Contact:	Meg Ricci USTR Computer Group (202) 395-4990
Reports Generated:	USTR, "Japanese Barriers to U.S. Trade"; and "Recent Japanese Government Trade Initiatives," November 1982, 75 pages

6. STR Foreign Trade Action Monitoring System (TAMS)

Contents:	Actions taken by major developed country trading partners that directly and indirectly affect U.S. exports and imports

Description: Citations of investigations, tariffs, surcharges, government procurement policies, quotas, standards and other measures, primarily NTBs, established in the industrialized nations compiled from Dept. of State, OECD, GATT and media sources

Not especially strong on high-tech industries

Available: Listings by country, including EEC, product, BTN number, action, date and source, and updates from sources used (updates available separately)

Contact: Meg Ricci
USTR Computer Group
(202) 395-4990

7. USTR Inventory of Selected Impediments to Trade in Services

Contents: Restriction on trade in services compiled by STR for latest GATT Ministerial meeting (1983)

Description: Industry by country, with a description of the impediment. Current as of late 1983

Available: Computer printouts by service industry, country imposing barrier, and description of the barrier

Contact: Meg Ricci
USTR Computer Group
(202) 395-4990

8. DOC Industrial Targeting Data Base

Contents: Targeting policies of twelve governments (Japan, Canada, FRG, France, Italy, Sweden, Brazil, Mexico, Taiwan, Korea, UK, and Singapore) in nine industries

Description: Computerized information for the following industries:

Telecommunications
Computers
Biotechnology
Semiconductors
Machine tools
Robotics
Aircraft
Pharmaceuticals
Space

Available: Unavailable before September 1985. May be restricted to government use only

Contact: Bob Sharkey
Office of Trade Information and Analysis/ITA
U.S. Dept. of Commerce
(202) 377-5675

9. DOC/NTB Inventory

Contents: NTBs, including barriers to trade in services. Very complete up to late 1970s

Description: Compiled for MTN negotiations in late 1970s with very thorough review of embassy reports, D&B Basic Information for Exporters. Revised through mid-1981

Available: Listings by country, NTB category, notifying country, intent, discriminatory effect, legal basis, significance for the United States and source

Notes:
1. May include some NTBs already negotiated away
2. The 1981 revision was not very thorough and most likely excludes some important NTBs
3. The inventory contains some classified negotiating information that is unavailable to the public

Contact: Dan Gardner
ITA
Room 3517
U.S. Dept. of Commerce
Washington, D.C.
(202) 377-3681

10. A. T. Kearney, International, Inc., Tokyo, Japan

Contents: Compilation of various Japanese NTBs and the products affected by them, including NTBs related to government procurement policies, government monopolies and pricing policies

Description: A good overview of the major manufacturing products affected by NTBs and what NTBs are used by Japan, although case studies and longer descriptions of specific NTB impacts are lacking

Report Generated: "Japanese Nontariff Barriers: A Selective Evaluation," final report, May 30, 1980, 158 pages

Appendix B
Agendas for Panel Discussions

AGENDA FOR CORPORATE DECISIONMAKERS' PANEL

Purpose

The purpose of this panel discussion is to involve corporate decisionmakers directly in our study concerning the impact of nontariff barriers on the high-technology strategies of U.S. companies. Corporate representatives have been selected from firms that have high-technology products that are likely to be subject to foreign trade barriers when they are exported. Their firms also are characterized by having significant corporate commitments to international markets. Representatives from these firms will be given the opportunity to offer judgments on questions concerning the manners in which their companies have adjusted to nontariff barriers.

Study Organization

This is the first of two panels. It will be composed of corporate decisionmakers in areas of research and development, marketing, international trade and overall corporate strategy. The second panel, on July 30, will be composed of U.S. government trade and R&D policymakers, as well as the government relations representatives from a sample of large multinational companies. They will be asked the same set of questions as the first panel, but with less emphasis on the impacts of NTBs on company decisionmaking and more emphasis on the impacts of NTBs on corporate strategy and on U.S. trade, investment and R&D policy goals. Agencies to be represented will include NSF, USTR and Commerce. Government relations representatives from the Washington offices of major U.S. companies will comprise the majority of the participants. The meeting will be held at NSF headquarters in Washington.

Format of the Panel

The discussion for the corporate decisionmakers' panel will be organized into seven parts:

1. Introduction of panel participants.
2. Presentation of format for the day's discussions.
3. Introduction of questions to orient the discussion.
4. Identification of NTBs in the foreign markets of participants' companies.
5. Panel discussion of specific impacts of NTBs on corporate decisions.
6. Advice on further research from panel members.
7. Summary of the panel's findings.

Format for the Discussion

For each of the major parts of the discussion, the background materials provided in Section 4, "The Impact of NTBs on Corporate Decisionmaking," will supply the questions to be discussed. Members of The Futures Group staff will introduce these questions. They will illustrate particular instances of NTB impacts on corporate decisionmaking by citing materials drawn from the case studies. Participants will then be asked to cite experience from their own firm's activities and those of other firms with which they are familiar.

The meeting will begin at 10 a.m., with a midmorning and midafternoon coffee break, as well as a short break for lunch.

Ground Rules

Our final report to NSF will not attribute specific comments and information to particular individuals and firms. We have followed this approach in constructing the case studies and believe the only way to promote a full and open discussion of this topic is to assure anonymity to all participants in the project and panel discussions.

Summary of Questions to Orient the Panel's Discussion

The primary focus of the discussion will be on how NTBs have affected corporate decisionmaking in the participants' firms.

The following questions provide examples of the type and range of issues we will address. These questions appear in greater detail in Section 4, "The Impact of NTBs on Corporate Decisionmaking."

- To what degree is the location of R&D determined by barriers in foreign markets, such as standards or government-enacted performance requirements?
- How sensitive is R&D to anticipated change in foreign technical requirements (for example, is modularization of the product undertaken in order to ease possible design changes)?
- What is the effect of barriers in certain markets on the R&D allocation to products that are intended for that market?
- How do firms respond in their export strategies to uncertainties in their foreign markets arising from NTBs?
- To what degree is market access dependent upon a firm's willingness to undertake direct investment or technology transfer in the host country?
- How effective are incentives tied to the host government's regional policy in encouraging firms to invest abroad?
- When some type of technology-sharing arrangement is required by the host government (either formally or informally), what are the factors that determine whether the technology will be licensed or the company will enter into a joint venture with a local firm?
- How do performance requirements such as specific export targets for manufacturing plants built locally affect the decision to undertake that investment?
- What is the effect of customs-related uncertainties (affecting delivery dates) on a company's export strategy, or are these difficulties eventually surmounted?
- How does a company remain competitive when it must deal with lengthy/costly certification procedures?

AGENDA FOR TRADE AND R&D POLICY PANEL

Purpose

The purpose of this panel is to bring U.S. government trade officials and corporate representatives together to discuss the effects of nontariff barriers (NTBs) on the international strategies of U.S. high-tech industries and on U.S. international economic policies. Corporate representatives are from high-tech firms subject to foreign trade barriers and committed to international markets. U.S. government trade officials have been drawn from offices within the Department of Commerce (DOC) and the Office of the U.S. Trade Representive (USTR) that are responsible for addressing trade issues in high-technology industries. Both corporate representatives and government officials will be given the opportunity to discuss and compare their perspectives on how nontariff barriers have affected corporate strategies, and how both the barriers themselves and U.S. corporate responses have influenced U.S. trade, investment, and R&D goals.

Study Organization

This will be the second of two panels. The first panel, which met on July 23 in New York, was comprised solely of corporate decisionmakers and focused on the effect of NTBs on corporate decisionmaking in the areas of R&D allocation and location, direct investment, technology licensing and export marketing. Information gathered from this meeting will be presented to the second panel on July 30. The results of both panels will be used to revise and extend our Interim Report for final presentation to NSF in mid-August.

Format of the Panel

The discussion will be organized into eight parts:

1. Introduction of panel participants.
2. Presentation of format for the day's discussions.
3. TFG staff summary of results for the Corporate Decisionmakers' Panel (July 23).
4. Introduction of questions to orient the discussion.
5. Panel discussion on policy issues arising out of the impacts of NTBs on corporate strategy in areas of R&D, investment, and exporting.
6. Panel discussion of NTBs identified during the study that are not adequately addressed by U.S. government trade agencies.
7. Advice on further research from panel members.
8. Summary of the panel's findings.

Format of the Discussion

For each of the major parts of the discussion, the background materials provided in Section 5, "The Impact of Nontariff Barriers on U.S. Policy," will supply the questions to be discussed. Members of The Futures Group staff will introduce these questions. Specific examples of NTB impacts drawn from the panel meeting on July 23 will be provided as a basis from which discussion on the effects of NTBs on corporate strategy and U.S. policy goals can proceed.

The meeting will begin at 10 a.m., with a midmorning and midafternoon coffee break, as well as a short break for lunch.

Ground Rules

Our final report to NSF will not attribute specific comments and information to particular individuals, firms or agencies. We have followed this approach in constructing the case studies and believe the only way to promote a full and open discussion of this topic is to assure anonymity to all participants in the project and panel discussions.

Summary of Questions to Orient the Panel's Discussion

The primary focus of the discussion will be on how NTBs affect corporate strategy and, in turn, American trade, investment and R&D goals. The following questions provide examples of the type and range of issues we will address. These questions appear in greater detail in Section 5, "The Impact of Nontariff Barriers on U.S. Policy."

- How can government officials obtain better and more up-to-date information on trade, investment, and/or R&D effects arising from NTBs, particularly when these impacts are not viewed by firms as requiring notification of government?
- What changes within the structure, or responsiveness, of government trade agencies should be considered in order to encourage American companies with trade-related problems to use official offices?
- Given a lack of complete information concerning NTBs, how can government trade officials determine which barriers in which industries must be immediately addressed?

- How can government trade officials respond more quickly and effectively to NTBs, once they have been identified?
- What is the relationship between performance-related barriers that stipulate and place requirements on new investments abroad and the cost structure of America's high-technology industries?
- If costs at home to investment and/or R&D are not raised significantly by these NTBs, then is improved knowledge of these foreign barriers important to the formulation of American R&D and investment policy objectives?
- If costs are significantly raised, then should the U.S. government more actively monitor and regulate the sourcing of investment and/or R&D abroad?
- What new barriers or technologies have arisen in recent years in which government attention is insufficient and, more importantly, can this situation be improved?

Appendix C Summary of the Corporate Decisionmakers' Panel on Nontariff Barriers to High-Technology Trade

MAIN FINDINGS

The panel found that while NTBs do not have many significant impacts on corporate decisionmaking, many companies, especially small- and medium-sized firms, face significant NTBs that impair their ability to compete in foreign markets. While smaller firms have to cut back on exports and sometimes seek larger partners to overcome constraints on sales due to NTBs, bigger firms face far fewer problems. Nevertheless, delays in certification, patenting and type approval for products and services, especially in Japan, do hamper larger firms. For the most part, these larger firms have representatives in host nations that are local nationals familiar with government officials and who can help the company get around the most detrimental impacts of NTBs.

In the opinion of the panel members, the Japanese are the most effective in using NTBs to protect their markets for local firms, in part because the Tokyo Round negotiations diminished the effectiveness of tariffs. Most saw the use of NTBs as directly related to Japan's world industrial leadership goals. Nearly all the panel members were concerned about the U.S. government's lack of information and expertise concerning NTBs and its inability to focus on negotiations concerning NTBs. Members recommended that special attention be focused on these shortcomings.

In the future, the panel's members proposed that government policymakers track, evaluate and focus negotiations on changes in NTBs in the EEC and Korea. It was felt that the support of these nations for telecommunications and biotechnology advances would increase their use of NTBs and require timely policy intervention.

DISCUSSION OF NONTARIFF BARRIERS

Standards

This discussion highlighted the fact that smaller firms face substantial problems in dealing with standards. A number of specific cases were raised, including FRG limits on the export of specific data items from a data base; FRG frequency standards for links to earth station equipment; and British restrictions on the resale of satellite links without having the British Telecom act as an intermediary. There was a general opinion that the data processing industry was more affected by standards than other sectors because the larger firms can use their market influence to impose NTBs that discriminate against other firms, both large and small, that use different standards.

It was felt that government-enacted standards do have an impact on R&D decisions when they are applied only to foreign firms, as is often the case in Europe. In a number of cases, Thomson-CSF, Siemens and their joint ventures face more liberal testing, verification and certification requirements than do foreign firms. In addition, the requirement that testing of U.S. high-technology goods be done in the United States and not in the nation mandating the testing imposes additional expenses for the U.S. firms, including the need to construct and maintain lab facilities.

The services aspect of high-technology industries is often more affected by standards that attempt to block market entry than is the hardware side. It was suggested that this occurs because services are often international in application and must therefore be provided in as many markets as possible. By limiting market access, governments can wring significant concessions from the providing companies. Consequently, a number of U.S. firms have formed alliances with systems houses in Europe to improve market access and ensure their compatibility with standards.

Panelists also felt that standards were employed to protect the monopoly market/structure enjoyed by many PTTs. At the same time, however, since high-technology fields such as telecommunications are subject to rapid change, it is difficult to maintain control. In fact, some cases were cited where the Japanese have established their own standard and are attempting to get it adopted by selling it to important developing nations, such as Brazil.

Yet, it was also noted that many developing countries have standards that, although they may act as de facto barriers to trade, are not intended as such. Many of these countries, for example, acquired telecommunications systems in the past that operate on standards no longer in widespread use. These countries are essentially locked into the standard, and must base new purchases on it. Such a situation, it was suggested, could provide small, flexible firms with a significant advantage over larger firms. Smaller firms are often better equipped than are larger firms to make quick decisions and provide customized products and services. Large, well-established firms may not feel the comparatively small size of these markets and warrant the extra effort required to adapt.

Government Procurement

Panelists generally believed that this barrier is inherent to most markets, although the objectives pursued through its implementation may differ among markets. Many of the NICs, for example, use their procurement markets as vehicles toward achieving their development goals. But developed countries, such as France, also use their procurement markets to develop or protect specific industries. Panelists did not find this barrier particularly damaging. Rather, it was simply considered to be common to most markets--including that in the United States--and one that can be addressed through joint ventures and technology licensing arrangements.

Investment Requirements

Panelists felt that foreign governments often have specific products they want produced and use investment requirements to achieve local production. Because of their potentially high cost, smaller firms often find it particularly difficult to operate under these NTBs. Local content requirements appear to be particularly troubling to smaller companies. Such requirements eliminate efficiencies-of-scale production and prevent cost-conscious smaller firms from making any significant attempts at market penetration. Several panelists argued that a more sophisticated staff within the U.S. government trade agencies is required to address these NTBs.

Investment-related NTBs are often promulgated by the departments of trade and industry within a government with specific developmental or protectionist objectives in mind. Panelists noted that the Ministry of Finance in most countries is often a potential ally to companies that face investment requirements (as these ministries are very concerned as to how efficiently scarce resources will be deployed), but that this avenue must be approached very carefully. Once a foreign company is caught between interministerial feuding, the company's interests will almost inevitably be damaged.

If the investment is made, the converse can be true. One company representative noted that his firm's sales in Japan fell by over 30 percent in only a few months due to his company's inadvertent marketing of bad products. Just at this time, however, the company began local production at a just-completed factory. Sales quickly rebounded to previous levels and have continued to grow since. The company representative noted that his company is perplexed as to how its market was able to collapse so quickly and drastically, and is equally uncertain how it suddenly rebounded just as new production facilities came on line. By whatever means, this company believes that local investment induced changes at the policy and distribution levels within Japan that boosted sales.

Perhaps the most vexing problem in regard to investment requirements is that, in many cases, the affected markets are crucial but not profitable. Both manufacturing and service industries serve customers that operate on an international scale. Banks, hotel chains, and large businesses (to name a few) generally purchase their data processing or telecommunications equipment from one company. This ensures compatibility and creates a constructive and efficient buyer-supplier relationship. This also requires the supplying companies to market their products in the geographic regions in which their customers do business--regions in which these suppliers might not ordinarily do business. One company representative claimed that, if his company were to suddenly abandon a full two-thirds of the country markets in which it now operates, it would lose perhaps 25 percent of gross revenues. The bottom line, the company's profits, however, would not be affected. This course of action, however, would sacrifice the profitable contracts that the company presently holds with major American companies that operate internationally.

Impacts of NTBs on Corporate Decisionmaking: On R&D

In regard to R&D decisions, NTBs have forced R&D facilities in some cases to be located in foreign markets as this was the only way to rapidly respond to changes in standards and other regulations. Such a presence provides U.S. firms with windows on opportunities in foreign markets. With some technologies, such as software, it was also easier to move R&D facilities abroad to respond to local demands because the costs of a software R&D facility are not great. They also permit U.S. firms to tap into foreign pools of talent.

There is pressure from local government to move R&D abroad. Some nations may raise import duties on needed parts or finished products unless royalties are steadily reduced through local R&D and production. These are generally called duty-uplift fees, and are in compliance with GATT regulations.

One panelist cited the efforts to which his company has gone in order to anticipate changes in the European market through local deployment of R&D facilities. For example, in Germany work councils made up of local company workers design ergonomic standards in order to improve working conditions for the company's entire work force. These standards may change virtually overnight, and may act as significant barriers to trade. This, however, is certainly not the objective of the work council. More significantly, American companies do not view these changing requirements as barriers, but as opportunities to expand market share. By locating R&D facilities in that country, this American firm can anticipate these changes and rapidly incorporate them into the relevant product.

There was a consensus within the panel that this is an area in which greater difficulties are anticipated. Company representatives agreed that the transfer of technology through local R&D requirements is a major concern within most American high-tech industries, and that this could become a major problem in attempting to operate in some of the NICs, for example. But panelists also noted that much of this locally conducted R&D flows back into the United States, and that much of the R&D located abroad is done for very legitimate reasons. Aside from the attractive incentives that many countries offer firms to conduct their R&D locally, there also is a natural and economical tendency within a company to base R&D as close to its markets as is possible.

On Marketing

Panelists contended that the Japanese were among the most consistent users of NTBs that affect marketing decisions. In instances where the Japanese require the disclosure of proprietary information, a U.S. firm will often attempt to avoid the Japanese market entirely, if possible. This is especially true when the processing technology required to produce high-tech products must be disclosed, rather than just information about the products themselves. As noted above, this alternative is not always viable as many companies are required by the nature of their contracts or services to operate in the Japanese market.

This was exemplified by concerns over disclosure of software that is used to run exchange systems in telecommunications.

If this software is deployed in Japan, it has to be licensed and the code disclosed publicly, while this would certainly not be required in the United States. One representative of a large firm noted how it took nine years for it to get a data services system set up and running in Japan. Although it finally succeeded, the impediments it faced led to its withdrawal from the market.

The risk in countries such as Japan is that U.S. firms may fail to gain any reward once they disclose their systems. Once the technology is licensed, new barriers may be erected to hinder the successful marketing of the relevant product or service.

Another panelist noted the difficulties in competing with state-owned concerns in marketing. For example, the French will often provide their large companies with access to capital at reduced rates. As a result, even when an American firm is able to come in with a competitive product at a low price, the financing arrangements the French company may offer are such that a contract with the company that is leveraged over a number of years will be less expensive in the end even if the original purchase price is significantly higher. This U.S. firm no longer attempts to compete in biddings in which French firms are participating. Marketing also can be affected by the need to disclose proprietary information prior to market entry. As noted above, this can be highly damaging, particularly as unrestricted market access is normally not guaranteed after the transfer of technology has taken place.

On Investment

One panelist noted that not enough attention is devoted to the barrier against investment, an NTB that has a very significant impact on service firms. In the cases of some services, it was felt that exclusivity arrangements that require a parent to give up ownership of a piece of its company to gain market entry were especially detrimental to competitiveness.

Buy-national policies of foreign governments were also criticized as preventing significant levels of investment in foreign markets. Firms are often warned by foreign government agencies that, once they reach a certain level of sales, new investments will be severely limited unless they form a joint venture with a host nation firm. In this case, firms are not normally averse to sinking additional investment into a country, unless that investment entails a significant transfer of technology as well.

Export performance criteria seem to concern panelists more than investment requirements. Host governments will often stipulate that, for market entry to be granted or a market expanded, the U.S. company must agree to produce locally a good in which a certain level will be exported. Often this is a good that the company already produces elsewhere, often in the United States, where economies of scale can be achieved. Unless production in the original facilities is reduced, the company will have to find additional markets for the now greater number of products it produces. Oftentimes firms will simply reduce production in their other facilities, but this raises overhead costs and impairs competitiveness.

On Exports

One of the major barriers in exporting, a panelist noted, is the desire by PTTs to have some type of control over foreign contractors. Even if U.S. firms bid in such a situation, they must commit themselves to a source of supply and thereby possibly lose the chance to opt for a better technology that may soon be marketed. Certification, particularly type approval, may readily be manipulated that allows host nation producers to put U.S. producers at a significant disadvantage vis-a-vis domestic suppliers. The generally accepted approach in addressing this NTB is, where it poses a significant obstacle, to create either a joint venture with a local company or set up a local office. As noted above, such an approach may discriminate in favor of larger, well-established firms that have the ability to finance a sizeable local presence.

Overall Recommendations

The overall opinion of the panelists was that further research should concentrate on studying policy responses to NTBs in three geographical regions. It was suggested that a few policy issues be given priority for a more detailed evaluation, relying on interviews with the key US. firms involved and broadening the study group to include major users of high-technology products (for instance, Citibank in the case of telecommunications) in addition to producers.

There was general agreement that more attention should be paid to NTBs in the EEC and Korea to better respond to problems that may arise as these nations attempt to employ NTBs to promote their high-technology sectors. It was the opinion of most panelists that U.S. dealings with Japan had not been very satisfactory in obtaining equal access to markets in a timely way.

Panelists believed that these regions should be specifically targeted by policymakers, through bilateral negotiations based on a quid pro quo arrangement. This would prevent Korea from using the Japanese approach in developing its industries (Korea was believed to be the next major player to emerge in high-technology trade), and give greater publicity to present NTBs in Europe and Japan. Particularly in the case of the latter, panelists stressed the need for greater publicity of those NTBs that the Japanese government has erected in order to curb imports and develop industries.

It was felt that the main policy objectives for government in addressing NTBs should be, first, obtaining market entry and second, establishing better negotiating mechanisms on NTBs. One panelist argued the geographic focus of attention should be on LDCs because they are the most rapidly growing new markets. Others argued for emphasizing negotiations with the EEC and Korea. Another approach was to target potential competitors of U.S. firms and track their behavior, particularly firms in the Pacific Rim.

It was felt that an additional study of NTBs would be useful only if it informed planning. Such a study should be in conjunction with a greater degree of direct government contact with the affected industries. Indeed, most panelists felt that Washington was poorly informed of most of the effects of those NTBs that their companies face.

SUMMARY OF THE PANEL ON GOVERNMENT POLICY AND NONTARIFF BARRIERS TO HIGH-TECHNOLOGY TRADE

Main Findings

Two contrasting views of the government's role dominated the panel's discussions. One emphasized the lack of oversight and sophistication of government, resulting in the United States selling its technology too cheaply, or being outsmarted by foreign governments and overseas companies. The other argued that although foreign governments target specific high-technology sectors for promotion, there has not been a major loss of U.S. firms' competitiveness through the use of NTBs.

Concern was expressed that U.S. high-technology firms were not very sophisticated when it came to confronting NTBs and recognizing their impact on the growth of their own business overseas. Some panelists felt that foreign governments were much more sophisticated in their use of NTBs, particularly since the reduction in tariffs achieved in the Tokyo Round negotiations left NTBs as the main trade policy device to use in promoting high-technology industries.

Concern also was expressed on the part of government officials that a number of high-tech industries had no clear constituencies opposed to harmful NTBs. These officials felt they were sometimes put in a difficult position because U.S. multinationals could solve their own policy-related problems abroad, while smaller, high-tech firms often lacked the resources and a vocal trade association to fight for their interests at the government level.

Multinationals had much more knowledge of foreign government bureaucracies and often had well-informed foreign nationals in their subsidiaries who have extensive experience in trade problems. As a consequence, they are able to cut deals with foreign nations and get around the problems created by NTBs.

Some government officials, however, still expressed concern that while some NTBs were a nuisance, others could have critical impacts on the competitiveness of U.S. high-tech companies. The latter NTBs, called killer NTBs by one panelist, are likely to be central to efforts by some foreign governments to promote specific high-tech sectors. These NTBs require a more sophisticated approach by U.S. policymakers, depending on the goals of the foreign nation that imposes them and the impact they will have on U.S. companies.

Several approaches to NTBs were suggested by the panelists. One was to let industry groups take over the U.S. response. Another was to create a sort of early-warning system in the government to initiate the dissemination of information about new NTBs that could harm U.S. firms. A third approach was to try to establish a global framework for the removal of NTBs.

A number of participants felt that not enough had been done to improve the way NTBs were removed. When Japan liberalized its telecommunications industry, there were no performance criteria established in the agreements reached by the U.S. Trade Representative with the government of Japan. However, a number of participants felt that the pressure in Europe to achieve more competitive high-tech industries would alleviate a number of the NTBs that had proved troublesome to U.S. firms.

On the other hand, several participants felt that the Europeans had become even more sophisticated in their use of incompatible standards to make it harder for U.S. firms to penetrate the EEC's markets, particularly in telecommunications. These panelists were concerned about the large size of several new telecommunications innovations that are about to be put in place over the next decade. These could be more affected by NTBs than something like a biotechnology system. In some cases, although U.S. products were more efficient, they could be excluded if they failed to conform to special European standards.

Some participants also believed that the roadblocks that hindered U.S. government action could be exacerbated by the shortening of the product life cycle for high-technology products. This makes government oversight more difficult and may increase the problems industry faces in determining the impact of NTBs.

Some approaches that were suggested to remove the roadblocks included: undertaking bilateral negotiations to remove the most troublesome NTBs; promoting direct industry-to-industry discussions when government initiatives seem inappropriate, and improving the bargaining capacity of U.S. negotiators.

Current Policy Issues

Two divergent views formed the basis for a contentious, but friendly, debate over the impact of NTBs on high-technology firms and the role of government policy. A number of other areas were debated. Some panelists believed that new technology firms would be much more aware of the problems posed by NTBs than their predecessors in the semiconductor and computer industries. Others thought that it was difficult to quantify the impact of NTBs on an industry, country or firm level, and that this task was being made more difficult because governments often changed NTBs to improve their effectiveness.

1. Government/Industry Interactions. One participant argued that the French were very interested in cooperation in improving entrepreneurship and innovation in their high-technology industries. They want to allow U.S. firms to make good deals and to have access to their market; to help meet the main French goals to increase industrial and academic collaboration and to improve competitiveness, through help from U.S. high-technology firms. This participant believed firms in emerging high-technology sectors would be more capable of avoiding an erosion of their technology lead than semiconductor firms were because they would be moving into new generations of technology very rapidly.

Several government officials feared that such a sanguine view of NTBs would lead to a repeat of the problems faced by U.S. semiconductor manufacturers in the early 1970s. Lack of sophistication led them to believe the Japanese were willing to cooperate in developing new technology. Most executives failed to recognize how much Japanese NTBs that closed the Japanese market to U.S. firms would affect their development. Such controlled access to the Japanese market was seen as a major reason why U.S. firms now face stiff competition from the Japanese. Safely behind a protected border, the Japanese firms, aided by targeted policies of their government, could develop their own products and profit from an often artificially stimulated indigenous demand under oligopolistic conditions. This facilitated an extension of the reach of these Japanese firms into the world marketplace.

This argument was supported by some government officials who warned that the situation is very different today from the 1970s. Foreign governments are now much more sophisticated in the use of NTBs. There are fewer tariffs and different criteria for NTBs. Patent filing problems have become more of a barrier. The Japanese are more sophisticated because they now use foreign investment in the United States to acquire access to emerging high-technology firms, largely cash-poor, venture-type firms from which they can license technology and transfer it to Japan more readily. For U.S. firms, one problem with the latter approach is that in Japan, large firms with substantial resources do much of the development and commercialization of high-technology products, while in the United States, small firms still are responsible for a sizeable part of these costs in high tech.

U.S. government officials now face problems because their scope for response is often limited because no clear constituency exists in some high-tech industries to support government initiatives. In addition, even when government plays a role intended to spark industry activisim, firms often break ranks to strike their own deals with foreign governments. This can result in some larger or more influential firms establishing terms that protect their own interests to the detriment of others. Sometimes, these deals can turn out to be albatrosses for companies that are not sophisticated enough to understand the inner workings of overseas markets. This has occurred when acquisitions by U.S. firms give them a role in companies in industries that are being squeezed by the host government.

On the other hand, one government observer argued that NTBs can be used to develop access to the U.S. market. A government, such as Japan's, can weaken NTBs to facilitate a U.S. firm's entry into its market, but can then use such a move toward more liberal trade policy to argue for greater access by Japanese firms to U.S. markets. This hidden agenda can provide a very meaningful way for Japanese firms to gain better access to new technology and to obtain a greater number of outlets for their own products.

2. The Scope for Government Action and Rival Government Industrial Policies. Some nations have explicitly linked trade policy to industrial policy. Some U.S. officials believe that government has been ahead of industry in identifying NTBs. But companies also feel frustrated with the government's lack of results. These very different interpretations of the role played by government seem to be tied to how one interprets trade theory. If one believes that comparative advantage will always win in the end, even when subsidies are employed by one government and not another, there is less likelihood one will be very concerned about NTBs. If, however, one is not convinced that competitiveness is driven largely by comparative advantage, but instead, believes that government subsidies or trade barriers can bring about shifts in competitiveness, a different approach to NTBs is required. One problem arising from this wide difference in orientation is that it obscures the approach the government should take toward policy in this area.

At the present time, most policymakers in Washington support the ruling ideology that comparative advantage determines competitiveness. Even accepting this, there are still important questions about what levels of pain can be accepted in terms of industrial distress that can be accommodated by U.S. firms. There also is the question of how NTBs and the trade strategies of our trading partners affect their role in negotiations. If others have a different objective in trade negotiations, perhaps U.S. policymakers should be thinking about achieving strategic trade advantages rather than focusing on free trade.

There is also the problem of who are the constituents of the government. Multinational corporations have more ability to grandfather arrangements with host governments. Other firms have less ability to cut deals with foreign nations. In addition, there is the question of just how the government goes about motivating firms to become more aware of trade policy problems. It has tried to educate firms, to do competitive assessments and to address industry groups. But its hands are often tied if there is a lack of unanimity among the firms in the industry.

The United States also faces problems because its trade policies are codified in a way in which many other nations' policies are not. Thus, legal considerations can be a dominant factor in the formulation of trade policy.

One government representative argued that one needs to have a realistic assessment of how far policymakers can go. Once this is established, NTBs can be categorized as nuisance NTBs, that can easily be removed, and killer NTBs that could prove very injurious to U.S. firms. How the United States approaches this problem, an industry representative suggested, may also depend upon the strategy of foreign governments. The Japanese usually want to develop indigenous firms, while the Koreans want to force U.S. companies to establish local operations. Another government suggested that tariffs had been a nuisance since their effect could be defeated easily. However, in Japan, NTBs proved more problematic since they were far more difficult to remove. In other situations, U.S. firms could make suggestions to foreign governments about how to improve the investment climate. An industry representative noted that what could be a nuisance to a large U.S. multinational could be death to a small firm.

Concern over how smaller firms could cope with NTBs was voiced by several participants. It was generally agreed that trade associations played an important role in improving information flow and exchange that was especially helpful to small firms. On the other hand, the lack of focus of U.S. policy goals was seen as a hindrance to smaller firms coping adequately with NTBs.

3. Remedies. Some remedies were suggested for the problems created in the past by ineffective government/industry relations in the face of NTBs. One is to have greater coordination of industry-level activity under the supervision of the private sector rather than the government. Another is to have the U.S. government initiate critical information dissemination to warn firms of impending changes in NTBs that will have a major impact on their business. A third opinion claimed that perceptions and policy lag reality; that U.S. policy needs to focus on the twin goals of promoting greater trade while at the same time seeking further liberalization of trade barriers through GATT.

NTBs and the Promotion of High-Technology Industries by Foreign Governments

A crucial factor promoting the growth of NTBs has been the desire by foreign governments to promote the growth of indigenous high-technology industries. Many nations seek to emulate Japan's success in the 1970s, particularly the European countries undergoing dynamic changes in their industrial structure.

This pressure has already led to a number of developments that are likely to increase the importance of NTBs as a policy issue. Among the most notable are the initiatives in the EEC to develop incompatible standards.

The EEC is now developing its own standards, especially in telecommunications. While there is an effort to get more participation in European markets by large U.S. high-technology firms such as IBM and AT&T, there is a clear tendency to establish policies to suit a technical standard such as X.25 and ISDN. A large, fixed telecommunications system, such as ISDN, may be more controllable and affected by NTBs than a biotechnology system.

European economies are likely to face great pressure over the next few years to get away from their balkanization in order to become more competitive. While this would meet U.S. firms' desires to have an internationalization of standards, based largely on the standards code, it also will erode the monopoly position of the European PTTs. This could lead the Europeans to rely more heavily on unique standards for their own EEC market, establishing a unique set of policy objectives in setting up its NTBs. It would be difficult to reconcile these goals with those of U.S. industry or government policymakers, especially if they were adjusted to contend with emerging technologies. It also would be difficult to penetrate the old boys' networks and to counter country--or EEC--designated favorites in foreign markets without a substantial change in the attitude of the business communities in foreign countries.

Opportunities for New Initiatives to Reduce the Use of NTBs

Industry representatives have argued that not much had been achieved in trade negotiations to remove NTBs. In telecommunications, the Japanese have been slow to liberalize procurement for their phone system, even after they had formally agreed to do so. It was felt that this reflected a failure to include performance criteria in the agreements reached by the USTR and too much of an emphasis on procedures. There also is frustration directed at the U.S. government for the way it has handled relations with Japan, problems in software valuation and procurement, and disagreements over arrangements with industrialized versus developing nations.

It was felt that the U.S. government should adopt accords on new standards that require specific changes in performance. Another participant argued that the standards issue is complex because it encompasses broader issues of discriminatory access to the certification of systems and acceptance of test results that require some tie to a broader policy toward NTBs. This is the case with software, where U.S. firms may not be able to compete due to their lack of compatibility with standards.

Some observers argued that if NTBs are removed, U.S. firms that are very strong in a technological sense can enter new markets and sell their products successfully. The problem is that, in some cases, such as telecommunications, deregulation results in increased competition and makes successful market entry by U.S. firms more difficult. Thus, a similar approach to the one taken for auto industry negotiations in Latin America could be more successful because it would set goals that are congruent with the aims of specific U.S. high-technology industries and seek to trade off access to U.S. markets for better entry into foreign ones.

However, this may require an industry consensus, a consensus among government agencies, and political leverage. Whether such a consensus for negotiations might be developed in the process of pursuing the negotiations themselves, as was the case in the Tokyo Round, is unclear. Government policymakers at the panel emphasized how it was difficult for them to initiate negotiations because some U.S. firms would not support talks to remove NTBs and because few trade associations focused attention on NTBs in high-technology areas.

The Need for an Early-Warning Mechanism

Policymakers were concerned about how to develop a way to respond to NTBs before their detrimental impacts became too widespread. In semiconductors, one pointed out, the problem had come and gone. Today's question is how to stretch out the process of oversight, how to view the problem. This is difficult since it is often very hard to assess the impacts of NTBs on the marketplace. Responding to NTBs may also be more difficult in the case of high-technology industries because there is not much appreciation of the fact that NTBs can have a big impact on these industries.

Another participant noted the disincentives that existed for the government to play a role in the removal of NTBs facing high-technology industries. First, it is difficult for the government to oversee what was happening because NTBs can change rapidly and there are always pressures to license new technology. Second, the government does not really have capable analysts, primarily because these analysts have no real power and few incentives to remain in their posts, as demonstrated by the rapid turnover in staff at key government agencies.

To resolve these problems, it was suggested that there be bilateral negotiations over the most troublesome NTBs. One participant noted that this had been tried in several cases over the past two years and had a positive effect on the negotiations over software valuation. In a sense, the U.S. government is moving in this direction with the U.S.-Japan High Technology Working Group.

The Need for Greater Compatibility of Standards and Procedures

Other initiatives that would be followed include having foreign countries accept testing done by U.S. firms in their U.S. facilities, especially where type acceptance is involved, and trying to establish interconnect procedures similar to those in force in the United States. In cases where an initiative by government has not been successful, as in Brazil, more direct industry-to-industry approaches ought to be considered. When U.S. industry representatives went to the U.S.-Brazilian Businessmen's Committee to discuss their concerns about the impact of Brazil's new telecommunications policy on U.S. firms selling to Brazil, they succeeded in obtaining changes where the U.S. government had failed.

While these approaches seemed useful, several problems were foreseen in taking such initiatives. First, one participant argued that each nation had a unique set of policy objectives in setting up its NTBs and it would be difficult to reconcile these goals with those of U.S. industry or government policymakers, especially since they were adjusted to contend with emerging technologies much of the time. Second, it was felt it would be difficult to penetrate the old boys' networks and to counter country-designated favorites in foreign markets without a substantial change in the attitude of business communities in foreign countries.

One participant argued that there were several changes that would improve the bargaining ability of U.S. negotiators: first, a sectoral perspective and a vision of how negotiations can have a significant impact on the sector. Second, stating negotiating objectives in terms of the results to be achieved rather than goals. Third, establishing a clear long-range strategy or set of goals for the United States. Fourth, providing a greater professional emphasis for U.S. negotiators, to reverse the current tendency to trade short-term gains for long-term because other nations have stronger negotiators than we do.

Appendix D
Panel Participants

CORPORATE DECISIONMAKERS' PANEL

James Clingham: Senior Counsel, RCA

Douglas Freeman: Specialty Monomers Project Manager, Phillips Petroleum

Irving Levine: Assistant Treasurer, International, NCR

Caesar Nerys: Director, Communications, International Data Processing

Kevin O'Neill: Director, R&D Planning and Finance, Prime Computer

Michael Phillips: Regional Director, Europe, Middle-East, Africa; Corporate Office of Multinational Operations, Motorola

Melvin Sallen: Vice President, Worldwide Sales, Analog Devices

Warner Sinbac: Manager, Telecommunications Affairs, General Electric

Frank Vince: Vice President, Product Strategy and Forecasting, Control Data Corporation

Christopher Vizas: Orion Telecommunications Ltd.

TRADE AND R&D POLICY PANEL

Government:

William Finan:	Senior Consultant, Technology Analysis Group (formerly Special Assistant to the Undersecretary for International Trade, Department of Commerce)
Clyde Prestowitz:	Counselor to the Secretary, Department of Commerce
Emery Simon:	International Economist, USTR
Bruce Wilson:	Deputy Assistant U.S. Trade Representative for Investment Policy, USTR

Industry:

Joe DeRose:	Program Director, Public Affairs, IBM
Dick Heimlick:	Vice President, Japanese Operations, Motorola
Lloyd Kaufman:	Senior Advisor, Charles L. Fishman, P.C.
Thomas Kern:	Manager of Systems Standards, Industry Standards Relations, NCR
Philip Onstad:	Special Assistant to the Senior Vice President, Control Data Corporation
Joseph Perpich:	Vice President, Planning and Development, Meloy Laboratories, Revlon Health Care Group
Joe Zycherman:	International Policy Advisor, AT&T Information Service

Appendix E
Case Studies

GOVERNMENT STANDARDS AS A BARRIER TO THE DELIVERY OF COMPUTER SERVICES IN EUROPE

A small U.S. telecommunications firm faced substantial difficulty in establishing itself in Germany. This was due to two problems related to standards. First, the German Bundespost would not give the firm frequency clearance for a downlink into Germany that would enable it to provide data services in Germany that were transmitted from a computer in the United States via a direct broadcast satellite or a packet-switched network. Second, the German government would not approve the data base the U.S. firm wanted to provide because of concerns about the export of sensitive data about the German economy.

The firm faced these barriers in spite of the fact that it offered a service that no one in Germany was offering. It felt there was great interest in seeing how it had managed to set up its system and was able to provide customers in Germany with everything from block mode or teletype (rather unsophisticated services) to an SNA gateway (a very sophisticated data gateway).

The firm felt that the German government was on a fishing expedition, that it was using standards to try to get the U.S. firm to team up with a German firm and then have the U.S. firm teach the German company what it was doing. The German government wanted the U.S. firm to put up all the capital and did not want to buy any of the R&D that the firm had already done in order to compensate it for its expenses.

The U.S. firm spoke to several German companies about such an arrangement and approached them about establishing a joint venture. Nevertheless, when it drew up the memorandum of understanding (MOU) necessary to incorporate, the German firms were unwilling to provide any commitments of capital. The U.S.

firm felt that even with a successful joint venture in place, it would have had no guarantee of access to the market.

The firm then approached the German Bundespost. An executive spoke with the head of the telecommunications policy section, recounting the barriers his firm faced. The representative of the Bundespost spoke with the potential joint-venture partners the U.S. firm had seen. Executives from these German firms then became resentful that the American executive had approached the government.

Because this U.S. firm can maximize its profits by expanding the use of the services it has designed, in order to get the R&D dollars invested in the product returned, standards and government requirements are key determinants of the firm's overall performance. Because standards such as those imposed by Germany forbid the firm from deploying a data base service without substantial modifications, and made it undertake major efforts to find a local partner, the firm's cost of business became too high and it could not operate in Germany.

It should also be noted that the firm had spent a considerable amount of time and funds before it sought to enter the German market developing a way to get around European standards that are incompatible with those established by the United States for satellite transmission. The United States uses 56 kilobit bandwidths, while the Europeans use 50 kilobits. This means there is a built-in incompatibility between U.S. and European systems at the physical interface level. The U.S. firm had to design new protocols to overcome this incompatibility.

Although it succeeded on a technical level, it was unable to convert its technical innovation into profits because of the pressure from the German government. Thus, standards can be linked with other NTBs, such as the need to approve a "downlink" and pressure to provide local firms with access to proprietary technology, to create an impossible situation for U.S. firms. This is especially true for smaller firms without local representatives who know how to get around the host government's regulations and how to utilize assistance from the U.S. government.

In addition, the firm's executives felt that the two years they had spent in developing the access technologies that permitted them to offer such a data base service in Europe had been wasted. They decided to refocus their efforts on the United States and Canada.

SALES OF U.S. FIRMS

A small U.S. software firm often bids on government RFPs for Western European nations. In many of these cases, it faces important national firms in the computer and computer services industry, such as Thomson-CSF or CIT-Alcatel, when turnkey combinations of hardware and software are requested.

The U.S. firm develops customized software to meet the specialized requirements of domestic and foreign corporations. It has found that when it attempts to compete with some of the larger European computer manufacturers that are also important providers of this type of turnkey equipment, it is extremely difficult to win important contracts. This happens because the European firms, especially those from France, are able to go to their governments and obtain cheap, long-term financing for the firms that want to purchase such turnkey systems. This has often been done at the very last moment, literally pulling the rug out from under the deals that the U.S. firms felt were wrapped up.

As a consequence, the U.S. firm is now very careful when it enters into competition against European firms for such turnkey systems. It often asks prospective buyers which other companies they are asking for bids. If the French firms are involved, the U.S. firm is likely to shy away from taking part in the competition for the sales because it does not want to waste staff time and travel and development money trying to make the sale, only to find that one of the French companies has come in with extremely low-cost, long-term government-assisted financing at the last minute, taking the contract away from all of the other competitors.

This occurs in spite of the fact that the software provided by the U.S. firm for the turnkey system is definitely a more sophisticated solution for the user, with a lower operating cost. Nevertheless, because of the government-assisted financing obtained by the French firms, the French competitors can argue that they are removing 5 to 6 percent from the total cost of the project by not forcing the purchaser to use market financing.

The U.S. firm feels that the French firms can use government-assisted financing in a very targeted manner. The executive who described this case depicted the French company as going back to the French government and saying, "We need a little more oomph on this one." This concern is reinforced by the belief that this type of government-industry cooperation is very ingrained in the French system and can easily be put into motion, while support for U.S. exporters from Eximbank is much more limited and takes more time to mobilize, except in the case of major contracts.

In addition, this executive felt that his firm's experiences, losing contracts in the face of strong foreign government financial assistance, had an impact on its R&D spending. The firm did not want to allocate funds for projects that it should compete for in Europe and other foreign markets. It feared that French firms could easily use government-backed financing to win contracts, even though the French software and turnkey systems were not as efficient and sophisticated as those provided by the U.S. company. It now feels there is no point in bidding on such contracts.

PROCUREMENT POLICIES ACTING AS A BARRIER TO EXPORT SALES

An earth station equipment company was informed by the Japanese government that procurement by NTT, the main Japanese telephone company, would be liberalized as a result of negotiations with the United States. A major project was being initiated by NTT for a development program that was expected to last five years or more. The program was for the construction of earth station equipment using very large scale integrated circuits (VLSI) products developed through an earlier government-sponsored program. The U.S. firm was eager to participate because entry into the program meant not only sales to the Japanese market but also an opportunity to learn some of the production techniques developed in Japan to use large-scale integrated circuits from the VLSI program.

The U.S. firm was advised that two contracts would be awarded by NTT for the development program, one to a Japanese firm and one to an American firm. The U.S. firm thought it had an excellent chance to win a contract because it was extremely competitive with the Japanese companies it faced in world markets and very much on the technological forefront of the industry. However, the price it bid on the contract was--according to NTT--considerably higher than that bid by NEC and by another Japanese firm. As a consequence, the two contracts were awarded to the two Japanese companies, in spite of the fact that the U.S. firm had been informed before the bidding was opened that one Japanese and one U.S. firm would be selected as contractors.

The U.S. company that bid on the contract believes it was misled. It is now much more reluctant to try to enter the Japanese market. Since it now has a market in the rest of the world that is much more lucrative, it has focused its energies on these non-Japanese, foreign opportunities. The firm, however, was especially disappointed because it competes with NEC on international tenders and wins its share. In other foreign markets, it has not had problems with its price being higher than that of NEC. The U.S. firm feels there may have been some special arrangements that enabled NEC to come up with a very low bid in Japan.

Representatives of the U.S. firm also feel that the Japanese did not want to let the U.S. company into Japan's market. Historically, NTT has worked very closely with NEC. The U.S. firm's executives had the feeling that NEC was very unhappy about two contracts being offered by NTT, especially because one was expected to go to a foreign competitor. The U.S. firm's staff surmised that because of NEC's concern, it had exerted considerable political pressure on the Japanese government and on NTT in order to have the contracts given to two Japanese firms. Although none of the U.S. firm's executives wanted to argue that the prices bid on the contract were linked to a desire to keep only Japanese firms in the bidding, there was an insinuation that things were very different in bidding for the Japanese market and in bidding for markets outside of Japan. The lower prices bid by Japanese firms for the Japanese contract were seen as related to a political strategy of wanting to keep non-Japanese firms from playing an active role in the development of new technologies. The fear motivating Japanese firms to act in this way, as it was perceived by U.S. executives, was that there might be an opportunity for non-Japanese firms to devise unique ways to adapt Japanese technologies that would give Japan's competitors advantages in international markets and in Japan's own market before Japanese firms had adequate time to develop similar products or other innovative products that would provide them with niches in critical markets. Thus, NTBs were seen as playing an important protective role, locking out the competition and giving Japanese firms more opportunity to exploit their own technological innovations.

In this case, the Japanese approach is very different from that taken by many U.S. firms. Historically, U.S. companies have been very eager to license new technologies very soon after they were proved to be commercially viable and to earn income from these innovations by letting foreign firms sell products based on such innovations. This may have grown out of a fear that short product life cycles in high-technology areas would reduce the opportunity for profit-making. However, another risk is involved with high-technology products. This risk is that licensees will be able to copy and adapt the product for their own markets and even for the markets of the licensor. This fear has come true in the case of the U.S. color TV industry and also in the case of U.S. semiconductor manufacturers, where licensing of state-of-the-art technology to the Japanese led to a rapid closing of technological gaps and, in the case of color TVs, an overtaking of U.S. firms. In software, however, U.S. firms have begun to behave differently and are often very reluctant to license state-of-the-art software to foreign firms, fearing they will lose control over the evolution of their product. This change of heart on licensing by firms in some of the newer high-technology industries may indicate that U.S. firms now recognize the real importance of controlling innovative technologies until they can achieve an important market position that is based upon their early introduction and continued ownership of new products. NTBs are one mechanism that can be used to assure such control, and discouraging foreign firms from entering key markets, such as those in Japan, through national firm-oriented procurement practices, is one way to promote indigenous development of what are considered critical technologies.

Another factor that may result in this type of behavior is the Japanese fear that strong U.S. firms will move rapidly to take over parts of the Japanese market if the pace of entry is not controlled. NTBs appear to serve as a means to control the pace of deregulation of the telecommunications market in Japan, in part because it is difficult to predict how the shift to more competitive procurement policies will affect the competitiveness of Japanese companies. To protect some of the larger firms against the impacts of deregulation, NTBs in areas such as procurement may be slow in coming down.

LICENSING RESTRICTIONS ADVERSELY AFFECT MARKETING AND DIRECT INVESTMENT OPPORTUNITIES

A major American electronics manufacturer maintains a small manufacturing and marketing presence in Brazil. This firm produces finished products in Brazil of a relatively low technology content. This firm also manufactures sophisticated systems of a high technology content in the United States, as well as parts and components for a variety of product lines. Some of these parts and components are required for the production of the low-end equipment produced in Brazil.

The Brazilian informatics market is monitored by the government's Special Secretariat of Informatics (SEI), which in 1979 assumed responsibilities for the data processing, micro-electronics, telematics and real-time control systems industries. Since then SEI's strategy has been to enhance the capabilities of national corporations in manufacturing complex technologies. SEI encourages foreign affiliates to produce state-of-the-art computer goods and services in Brazil (both for local consumption and export), as well as to construct and improve local R&D facilities. Once a product line can be manufactured with local capital, the market is protected to give the infant industry an opportunity to develop. Foreign producers, who may have initially brought this technology into Brazil, are encouraged to move into more sophisticated products. Further development of the original product line is thus left to Brazilian manufacturers. As a result of this, imports are monitored through a licensing regime which enables the government to reduce or stem the flow of foreign-produced parts and components into the country once a local manufacturing capacity is developed.

This American company has not been successful in obtaining import licenses in Brazil for its sophisticated systems, and over the past eighteen to thirty-six months has faced delays in obtaining licenses both for parts and components and for finished products of a low-technology content. The Brazilian government has informally intimated that import licenses for both low- and high-tech systems could be more readily obtained by this company if it were to develop local manufacturing capacity for the more sophisticated systems, and perhaps conduct greater levels of R&D in the country. Apparently the government presently believes that this company's current production, at the low end of the technology scale, does not significantly add to the productive base of Brazil's informatics industry, does not significantly add to export volume, and does not substantially contribute to the Brazilian efforts to build a local industry.

Although it is not certain, it appears that the two American market giants in Brazil, IBM and Burroughs, have been successful at obtaining import licenses for their equipment and parts in recent years. Together these two control a sizeable share of the Brazilian market and employ several thousand workers. Moreover, roughly eight years ago the Brazilian government attempted to deny import licenses to IBM. The resulting bottlenecks and shortages almost brought the automated capacity of the country--and the government--to a standstill. IBM was quickly reissued licenses.

Delays and difficulties in receiving import licenses for the parts and components necessary to produce low-technology equipment have led this company to scale back operations in Brazil. Generally the delays stem from an apparently arbitrary determination by the Brazilian bureaucracy as to whether licenses will be issued. The company is unable to explain why some licenses are denied, while others are granted soon thereafter. The difficulties arise from the financial arrangements stipulated by the Brazilian government. Currency restrictions are imposed, and the company is required to hold cruzeiros (the local currency) for extended periods at a time of high inflation. Moreover, given the present financial difficulties of the country, there is no guarantee that the cruzeiros will indeed be exchanged for dollars. As a result of these and other problems, the company is steadily reducing production and employment in its local operations. The Brazilian government has not, up to the present, shown any willingness to ease its terms and issue the range and number of import licenses necessary for a profitable and growing business for this company in Brazil.

PATENT RESTRICTIONS RESULTING IN LOSS OF ACCESS TO MARKETS

A U.S. company developed a new telecommunications product that it patented in the U.S. in 1970 and in Europe in 1971 to 1973. It was unable to receive a patent on the product in Japan because, in the company's opinion, the Japanese wanted to develop their own product as an integral part of Japan's strategy in telecommunications.

The U.S. firm commercialized the product through joint ventures with Siemens and others in the EEC and tried to sell it in Japan in the early 1970s to NTT, the Japanese phone company. NTT refused. In order to get into the Japanese market, the company tried to form a joint venture with Japanese partners, but the Japanese companies said that NTT would not approve of such an arrangement. Consequently, the product was developed in Japan by a Japanese firm.

The U.S. firm believes the Japanese infringed on its patent rights and used Japan's refusal of a patent to keep it out of the Japanese market. The U.S. firm has begun suits against the Japanese company for selling its product in foreign markets where the U.S. firm holds patent rights. The U.S. firm has had some favorable rulings supporting its case; however, it does not believe this is an effective remedy for protecting its technological competitiveness.

The U.S. firm has concluded that despite NTT's recent willingness to open bidding on telecommunications products to foreign firms, it has systematically used the refusal to patent new products to deny entry into Japan while using a protected home market to develop a competitive product similar to that produced in the United States. The U.S. company reached this conclusion because, during the late 1970s, NTT was paying Japanese firms more to manufacture the product than it would have cost to buy it from the U.S. firm. Thus, the Japanese price was subsidizing product development by Japanese firms.

Subsequently, Japanese companies started to market this product in slightly different form in the United States for 30 percent under the market price. As a result, the U.S. firm has now lost sales in the U.S. market and is using several legal avenues to gain restitution.

GOVERNMENT PROCUREMENT POLICIES LIMIT SALES OF TELECOMMUNICATIONS AND AFFECT MARKETING AND R&D ALLOCATION

A subsidiary of a major Fortune 500 firm sells a telecommunications product to a small number of foreign governments. Because these governments are very interested in having telecommunications technology transferred to their own national companies, they often purchase just the components rather than the final product, and their buy-national policies have for all practical purposes closed off their markets to final product sales. As a consequence, the U.S. firm, which in the absence of discrimination would conduct R&D targeted at foreign sales, will allocate little or no R&D funds to becoming a leader in the telecommunications technology required abroad, concentrating instead on sales to the U.S. market and innovative projects that can be funded by the Department of Defense. It may be unrealistic to expect that the firm would devote substantial funds to foreign markets now, since U.S. markets are growing so rapidly. It is, however, likely that this firm would focus on foreign markets once U.S. growth stabilizes if there were no discrimination. The firm also has developed unique marketing practices to obtain component sales abroad, working through trading companies in Japan and industrial partners in Europe.

The NTBs faced by this firm are largely the result of national policies to promote the growth of selected high-technology sectors. While the telecommunications product it sells is difficult to market abroad, because of closed government procurement markets, selecting only national firms for sales, the U.S. firm plays an important role as an original equipment manufacturer (OEM), or component supplier, for foreign companies. Because of its expertise, it participates in joint ventures with foreign companies since it knows how to lower the costs of producing the final product and is expert in managing production, thus lowering the risks of producing faulty products.

This situation is somewhat relaxed when the final product is procured by a quasi-government agency or an entity that is more independent of existing government controls. In such cases, the U.S. firm's final product is more likely to win in competitions with products of foreign companies because of clear advantages in price and performance. However, there has been at least one case where a much smaller foreign component firm has won a competition with the U.S. company because of its familiarity with the standards requirements of a Western European government.

Nevertheless, a company executive believes that since the number of buyers for the final product is extremely small, governments do not have to establish a broad range of NTBs. Rather, they can utilize a buy-national approach that leads agencies and national companies to buy only components and not the final product. The governments appear to assume that the benefits of this policy far outweigh the liabilities, because employment is being generated in high-technology sectors and important skills are being developed in national firms. There are some differences among governments where purchases of U.S. goods are more likely because of deregulation of state PTTs. The more independent the new authorities are from the state, the more likely they are to purchase U.S.-produced products.

As a consequence of these policies, the U.S. firm does not do any R&D for overseas markets, and exports only products developed in the United States. While the U.S. company could do research that would put it in a key position in foreign markets because of the complexity of its product and the details of producing it, it has not. Rather, it focuses on innovative products required by U.S. customers. Recently, it developed an innovative power supply that has been marketed to an international agency and then sold abroad. However, when the U.S. firm plans its own R&D program, it does not target anything for the Japanese, European, and developing nations' markets, where it has little potential for business. Instead, it tries to trigger U.S. government funding for innovative products, often from the Defense Department.

The U.S. firm has also altered its marketing practices because of the buy-national practices it faces. It obtains some sales through lobbying various PTTs to get international communications agencies to purchase its final products. But another large part of its sales comes from component sales to foreign companies that are often made through a joint venture or trading company. In England, Italy, West Germany and France it works through OEM partners; in Japan, through a trading company.

This marketing approach has required the U.S. firm to have a separate set of marketing capabilities overseas. It has developed a separate marketing staff that entails greater expense. It also believes that in order to respond to the NTB, it must have staff that understands international finance and is sensitive to foreign customers. The firm feels this staff would not be required without the NTB since it leads the world in the telecommunications products it makes.

Many foreign companies are especially interested in acquiring the project management skills the U.S. firm employs in producing its final product. As a consequence, the firm has been asked to license some of its technology in Japan before it can obtain sales. It has also participated in a U.S. government-sponsored program with an LDC where a local company's staff participated in the assembly of the U.S. firm's final product in order to gain familiarity with the U.S. company's project management skills. Once such arrangements are established, there are usually few barriers to component sales to a nation.

The U.S. firm also benefits from the name-recognition of its parent in dealing with foreign governments. Given the complexity of its product, the firm can set foreign customers and foreign governments at ease because of its parent's reputation.

However, the executive interviewed believed that its parent's failure to emphasize marketing sophistication sometimes placed it at a disadvantage internationally. He cited the ease with which IBM operates in many of the markets that are often closed or restricted when his firm tries to enter them. He felt that IBM's focus on marketing had led to its successs abroad, especially since it was able to explain to foreign customers and foreign governments why their products were needed and how their products could fit into the plans of these clients. In essence, IBM understood how to project these needs in foreign markets and had succeeded admirably. Other firms, like his own, were just beginning to learn how to do this.

STANDARDS AND PROCUREMENT AFFECT MARKETING, SALES, AND R&D

A major American manufacturer of computer and communications equipment encountered unexpectedly severe difficulties in bidding on new data communications contracts in the European market. A new packet switching protocol, the X.25, had been under development for several years by private industry in both the United States and Europe. This company anticipated that the adoption of this new protocol in Europe would be gradual, that is, that initially only pieces of a communications system (peripherals) would have to be supported by the protocol.

To the surprise of many foreign producers, the European PTTs did not opt for the gradual adoption of the X.25, but made it the protocol for the entire communications system. As a result, foreign competitors who had not yet developed equipment compatible with the X.25, like this American company, were kept out of the market. The PTTs may have had several reasons for stipulating that the X.25 support entire systems. Most European manufacturers were ahead of their American counterparts in developing the requisite equipment; once the X.25 became the standard for the industry, the only qualifying suppliers were predominantly European. Moreover, the market giant, IBM, utilized a different architecture, SNA. By requiring all equipment to support the X.25, the PTTs may have hoped to give their own industries a significant share of this market before IBM could bring its own product lines into conformance with X.25.

Development of the equipment compatible with this protocol became a top priority in the American company's R&D facilities in the U.S. (where all of its R&D is conducted). Because of the technical complexity of the design, this company deemed a licensing arrangement with a European concern that had already developed the equipment as inappropriate. The equipment, in any case, would have to be modified to be compatible with the American company's. Such modifications would be complex, and would require personnel who were familiar with the X.25's design characteristics. For this reason, development of compatible equipment was undertaken as an in-house project.

Company personnel operating in the European market were brought home to expedite the development process and ensure compatibility with the European standards. As technical requirements for the protocol differed somewhat among the major European markets, the American company chose to modularize the design so that slight modifications could be made to suit each market.

Before marketing could begin, the product was subject to a rigid certification process. Moreover, type-certification (where once the model or design is certified, testing is not required on each individual and identical piece of equipment) was unavailable to imported equipment; rather, each time the product was brought into the country, it had to undergo new testing. This contrasted with the requirements facing local manufacturers such as Honeywell-Bull or Siemens, which were not required to certify each item individually as it was brought to market. An executive at the American company stressed that this was a cumbersome but relatively minor barrier that all exporters faced and that could be anticipated.

Far more serious is the issue of government procurement, a major problem in marketing equipment (even after it is compatible with the X.25 protocol) in the French, German, and English markets. This company has been unable to significantly penetrate the government procurement markets in Europe, despite the claims of these governments that they are accepting bids from all qualified firms. As do almost all U.S.-based companies, this firm addresses this barrier in bilateral fora, that is, between itself and the relevant government. A strong marketing presence in these countries is used to build contacts with representatives of government and business. Moreover, many of the smaller European companies have offered their assistance in helping this and other

American firms penetrate the government procurement market. These European companies fear that, should the American firms be kept entirely out of this market, they would retaliate by refusing to license American technologies to the Europeans. This would be particularly damaging to the smaller European companies that are often dependent upon licensed technologies.

Nevertheless, many of the market giants in Europe, such as Siemens or Honeywell-Bull, would welcome the opportunity to become the IBM of their market. These firms believe that if American companies were cut off from the European government procurement markets entirely, American technologies would be licensed to these European concerns as the only viable method of maintaining an American presence in the European procurement market. As a result, this American firm is willing to devote considerable resources to maintain a presence to lobby against the rise of nationalistic commercial policies.

EFFECT OF NTBs REDUCED THROUGH LOCAL PRESENCE IN FOREIGN MARKETS

An American electronics manufacturer with marketing presences in Japan and Western Europe has faced few difficulties in these markets that can be directly ascribed to nontariff barriers. Acting on the belief that most of the difficulties that would be encountered in these markets would be based on, or exacerbated by cultural factors, the company has staffed its entire overseas offices with local nationals.

The company has manufacturing presences in the United Kingdom and Japan, each with roughly 200 employees, none of whom are American. The managers and technicians in these foreign offices, being local nationals, are brought to the United States to be acquainted and trained with the company's policies and operating procedures. Investment in these foreign manufacturing operations was undertaken for a variety of reasons, chief among them being financial and labor considerations. Attractive investment incentives are provided through the regional policies of various European countries, while access to a technically trained labor pool is often an important prerequisite to direct investment. Occasionally a strong incentive in one area will offset a disadvantage in the other; for example, significant financial assistance would mitigate the added expenses required to provide the necessary technical training to an inexperienced labor pool. This company confronted this situation in Ireland, where it subsequently constructed R&D facilities. American nationals were brought over to help train Irish employees in the relevant technologies.

An executive at this company made clear that, while his company does face nontariff barriers in the European and Japanese markets, the significance of these is overshadowed by cultural factors which inhibit market development. For example, the company's greatest problem with its Japanese manufacturing and marketing operations is staffing. Given the traditional nature of Japanese employment, with long-term responsibilities incumbent upon the Japanese employer, this American firm found it difficult to attract qualified local personnel. Experienced Japanese employees are reluctant to change employers at mid-career, especially to a foreign firm only recently established in the country. In the end, this company chose to hire young Japanese graduates at the beginning of their careers, train them for six months in the United States, and return them to manage the company's Japanese operations. The short-term cost incurred in using relatively inexperienced personnel was believed to be offset in the long-run through the development of a subsidiary staffed by nationals and experienced in market development. The company anticipates that it may require 20 years of operation for this subsidiary to fully develop its potential.

STANDARDS AS BARRIERS TO MARKETING AN INNOVATIVE BIOTECHNOLOGY PRODUCT

A large U.S. biotechnology firm has concerns that it will find it difficult to sell its products in France because of product testing restrictions being proposed by a number of agencies in the French government that will make organizing a distribution network in France very cumbersome. It has hesitated to proceed with licensing arrangements because its licensee cannot establish a stable distribution network because of possible testing bottlenecks. It may wait to see if another, larger firm will take over its marketing.

The restrictions that are likely to be imposed by the French government would check for the safety and performance of diagnostic products. The entry of non-French biotechnology products into the French market will likely be limited by such testing, not because of any failure to conform to French standards, but because the testing limits the timeliness with which the French licensee could supply its customers with products they require.

The testing really constitutes a barrier to establishing the distribution network required to market a new product. The French licensee of the U.S. firm has found that the new regulations would make it extremely difficult to set up a distribution system. Without being able to guarantee a timely flow of product to distributors, the licensee cannot get enough firms to sign up to establish a distribution network for the U.S. firm. The U.S. firm has not pursued finding a way to sell in France, but is considering trying to get a large, multinational firm to take over its foreign marketing because it could deal with such marketing problems more effectively.

List of Abbreviations

BT	British Telecom
CDC	Control Data Corporation
DOC	Department of Commerce
EEC	European Economic Community
GATT	General Agreement on Tariffs and Trade
GOF	Government of France
GOJ	Government of Japan
IC	Integrated circuit
ISO	International Standards Organization
JIS	Japanese Industrial Standards
KDD	Kokusai Denshin Denida
MITI	Ministry of International Trade and Industry
MOU	Memorandum of understanding
MPT	Ministry of Post and Telecommunications
MTN	Multilateral trade negotiations
NTB	Nontariff barrier
NTT	Nippon Telegraph and Telephone Corporation
OECD	Organization for Economic Cooperation and Development
OEM	Original equipment manufacturer
PTT	Post, Telephone and Telegraph
R&D	Research and development
RFP	Request for proposal
SEI	Special Secretariat of Informatics
TI	Texas Instruments
UNCTAD	U.N. Conference on Trade and Development
USTR	U.S. Trade Representative
VAN	Value-added network
VDE	German Society of Engineers
VLSI	Very large scale integrated circuit

Bibliography

Abelson, Donald. Director, Technical Trade Barriers, USTR. Interview, May 17, 1984.

Baldwin, Robert E. Non-Tariff Distortions of International Trade. Brookings Institution, 1970.

"Bizarre Standards Confusion." Financial Times (March 5, 1984).

Bortnick, Jane. International Telecommunications and Information Policy: Selected Issues for the 1980s. Washington, D.C.: U.S. Government Printing Office, 1983.

Braggaar, Hans. "European Antitrust Case Against IBM Still on Books." Computer World (April 30, 1984).

"British Telecom Connects with the Retail Industry." New Scientist (November 26, 1981).

Bronson, Donald R. President, Federated Technology and Electronics Corporation, New York, a former employee of RCA-France. Interview.

Electronic Industries Association. "Changes in U.S. Telecommunications Industry and Impact on U.S. Telecommunications Trade." Submission to the International Trade Commission, April 17, 1984.

"Europe's Computer Groups Forge Pact." Financial Times (March 16, 1984).

Farnoux, Abel. Excerpts from the Report by the Committee for Electronics. Paris: French Ministries of State and of Research and Technology, March 1982.

"Foreign Test Data To Be Accepted." Journal of Japanese Trade and Industry (May/June 1984).

"France Blends Technology, Socialism." High Technology (November 1983).

General Accounting Office. Assessments of Bilateral Telecommunications Agreements with Japan, October 7, 1983.

"IBM and Mitterand--An Entente Cordial. Financial Times (November 28, 1983).

Inside U.S. Trade (March 9, 1984).

Inside U.S. Trade (September 5, 1983).

International Trade Commission. Foreign Industrial Targeting and Its Effects on U.S. Industries, Phase I: Japan, October 1983.

Japan Economic Institute. "Japan's Satellite Development Program." JEI Report (March 16, 1984).

Japanese Standards Association. Ministry of International Trade and Industry. JIS Guide 84, Part I, p. 5.

Kaufman, Lloyd, Senior Advisor; Fishman, Charles L., P.C., Washington, D.C.; and Zycherman, Joseph, International Policy Advisor. AT&T Information Systems, Morristown, New Jersey. Discussions.

Kearney, A. T., International, Inc. Japanese Non-Tariff Barriers: A Selective Evaluation. Tokyo: Kearney Management Consultants, May 30, 1980.

Knickerbocker, Frederick. Oligopolistic Reaction and Multinational Enterprise. Boston, Mass.: Graduate School of Business Administration, Harvard University, 1973.

Knight, Frank H. Risk, Uncertainty and Profit. New York: Harper & Row, 1965.

The Labor Industry Coalition for International Trade. Performance Requirements. Washington, D.C.: LICIT, 1981.

Liser, Florizelle. USTR. Interview, May 17, 1984.

"Miami Lab to Certify U.S. Goods for Sale in Japan." New York Times, May 23, 1984.

"Non-Tariff Barrier Analysis." Computerized data base maintained through 1977 by USTR.

Schott, Jeffrey. "The GATT Ministerial: A Postmortem." Challenge (May/June 1983), pp. 40-45.

Semiconductor Industry Association. The Effect of Government Targeting on World Semiconductor Competition, January 1983.

Shark, David. Director of Government Procurement, Office of GATT Affairs, USTR. Interview, May 17, 1984.

Shelp, Ronald K. Beyond Industrialization: Ascendancy of the Global Service Economy. New York: Praeger Publishers, 1981.

Spero, Joan. "Information: The Policy Void." Foreign Policy, No. 48 (Fall 1982), pp. 139-156.

United Nations. Centre on Transnational Corporations. Transborder Data Flows and Brazil: A Case Study. New York: United Nations, 1983.

U.S. Congress. House. Committee on Government Operations. International Data Flow. Testimony of Hugh P. Donahue of Control Data Corporation.

U.S. Congress. House. Committee on Government Operations, Subcommittee on Government Information and Individual

Rights. International Data Flow. Washington, D.C.: U.S. Government Printing Office, 1980.

U.S. Congress. House. Committee on Interstate and Foreign Commerce, Subcommittee on Communications. International Barriers to Data Flows: Background Report. Washington, D.C.: U.S. Government Printing Office, 1979.

U.S. Congress. Senate. Committee on Commerce, Science and Transportation. Long-Range Goals in International Telecommunications and Information: An Outline for United States Policy. By the U.S. Department of Commerce. National Telecommunications and Information Administration. Washington, D.C.: U.S. Government Printing Office, 1983.

U.S. Congress. Senate. Committee on Government Operations. International Information Flow: Forging a New Framework. Washington, D.C.: U.S. Government Printing Office, 1980.

U.S. Department of Commerce. International Trade Administration, Office of International Sector Policy. "An Analysis of Automobile Local Content Laws in Other Countries," October 1983.

U.S. Department of Commerce. International Trade Administration. The Computer Industry, April 1983.

U.S. Department of Commerce. International Trade Administration. The Telecommunications Industry, April 1983.

U.S. Department of Commerce. International Trade Administration. Technical Barriers to Trade, Vol. 4, September 1981.

U.S. Department of Commerce. International Trade Administration. Government Procurement, Vol. 2, July 1981.

U.S. Special Trade Representative. Report to the U.S. Congress on the Agreement on Technical Barriers to Trade--Standards Code, January 1980/December 1982.

U.S. Tariff Commission. A Report on Non-Tariff Trade Barriers to the U.S. Senate, Committee on Finance. Washington, D.C.: U.S. Government Printing Office, 1974.

U.S. Trade Representative. Interviews with officials, April/May 1984.

U.S. Trade Representative. "Selected Problems Encountered by U.S. Service Industries to Trade in Services." Computerized listing, May 11, 1983, p. 49.

U.S. Trade Representative. Japanese Barriers to U.S. Trade and Recent Japanese Government Trade Initiatives, November 1982.

U.S. Trade Representative. A Preface to Trade, 1982.

U.S. Trade Representative. "International Trade Issues in Telecommunications, Data Processing, and Information Services." Unpublished.

Vaughan, Beverly. International Economist, USTR. Interview, May 17, 1984.
"When the Planning Has To Stop." New Scientist (December 2, 1982).